HEALING THE CHURCH

DIAGNOSING AND TREATING THE CLERGY SEXUAL ABUSE CRISIS

SISTER NUALA KENNY, OC, MD, FRCP(C)

© 2012 Novalis Publishing Inc.

Cover: Blair Turner
Layout: Audrey Wells

Published by Novalis

Publishing Office
10 Lower Spadina Avenue, Suite 400
Toronto, Ontario, Canada
M5V 2Z2

Head Office
4475 Frontenac Street
Montréal, Québec, Canada
H2H 2S2

www.novalis.ca

Library and Archives Canada Cataloguing in Publication

Kenny, Nuala P.
    Healing the church : diagnosing and treating
the clergy sexual abuse crisis / Nuala P. Kenny.

Includes bibliographical references.
ISBN 978-2-89646-470-8

    1. Child sexual abuse by clergy. 2. Child sexual
abuse--Religious aspects--Catholic Church. 3. Catholic
Church--Clergy--Sexual behavior. 4. Healing--Religious
aspects--Catholic Church. I. Title.

BX1912.9.K45 2012   261.8'3272088282   C2012-903406-1

Printed in Canada.

The Scripture quotations contained herein are from the New Revised Standard Version
of the Bible, copyrighted 1989 by the Division of Christian Education of the National Council
of the Churches of Christ in the United States of America, and are used by permission.
All rights reserved.

All rights reserved. No part of this publication may be reproduced, stored in a retrieval system,
or transmitted in any form, or by any means, electronic, mechanical, photocopying, recording,
or otherwise, without the written permission of the publisher.

We acknowledge the financial support of the Government of Canada through the Canada Book Fund
for business development activities.

5 4 3 2 1   16 15 14 13 12

CONTENTS

Foreword by Archbishop Anthony Mancini 5

Personal Preface
My Journey: From Diagnosing Children
to Diagnosing Sins Against Children 13
The Early Work on Clergy Sexual Abuse. 14
Unfinished Business. 17

Introduction 21

Chapter 1
The Pain and Suffering of Clergy Sexual Abuse 27
Objectives 28
1. The Pain and Suffering of Sexual Abuse of Children and Youth by Clergy 29
The Dynamics of Sexual Abuse by Clergy. 33
3. Gospel Themes that Propose an Alternative. 36
4. Some Questions for Reflection and Action 37

Chapter 2
A History of the Problem. 39
Objectives 40
1. Some History 40
2. Leadership Response: Identifying Patterns and Themes. 46
3. Gospel Themes that Propose an Alternative. 50
4. Some Questions for Reflection and Action 51

Chapter 3
Mechanisms of Disease and Accurate Diagnosis 53
Objectives 54
1. The Nature of the Crisis. 54
2. Assessing Some Proposed Remedies. 57
3. Gospel Themes that Propose an Alternative. 63
4. Some Questions for Reflection and Action 64

Chapter 4
The Anatomy of the Crisis: Relationships, Power and Clericalism 65
Objectives 66
1. The Culture and Structure of the Church 66
2. Clericalism and Its Role in the Abuse Crisis. 71
3. Gospel Themes that Propose an Alternative. 75
4. Some Questions for Reflection and Action. 76

Chapter 5
Flesh and Blood: Moral Theology and a Theology of Sexuality 77
Objectives 78
1. Sexuality in the Catholic Tradition 78
2. Moral Theology and a Theology of Sexuality 83
3. Gospel Themes that Propose an Alternative. 86
4. Some Questions for Reflection and Action 87

Chapter 6
Prescription: A Re-evangelization of the Church. 89
Objectives 90
1. The Health of the Church 90
2. Elements in Any Effective Prescription. 94
3. Gospel Themes that Propose an Alternative. 98
4. Some Questions for Reflection and Action 99

Some Thoughts and Prayers Regarding Prognosis. 101

Appendix I: Early History of Sexual Abuse by Clergy. 103

Appendix II: Some Key Modern History 104

Endnotes 107

Bibliography 118

FOREWORD

I have read Sister Nuala Kenny's book and found it very instructive and challenging. As a doctor, her experience and modus operandi is evident in the structure and process of her approach to the issue of sexual abuse by clergy and religious in the Church. Her diagnostic concerns are clear. For one who is not a doctor, this way of presenting, analyzing and understanding the issue of sexual abuse is very helpful. My remarks therefore reflect how I, as a bishop struggling with this crisis of sexual abuse, respond to Sr. Nuala's diagnosis, criticism and prescriptions.

Central to this diagnostic approach is a desire to deal with and treat the real problem with the best that we have, in order to restore the Body of the Church to optimal health. It is very instructive to see that, if the presenting problem is not fully and adequately understood, then the proposed ways of attending to it will be inadequate; at the very least, only the symptoms are treated, and at the very worst, more damage can be caused. As a bishop trying to find a way forward in this matter, I receive Sr. Nuala's words as a call to more effectively exercise my role.

So what is the problem and cause of sexual abuse? This question is central to the challenge of Sister Nuala's reflection. She argues that at the heart of the present Church's way of being there is something fundamentally wrong. The matter of sexual abuse in the Church is not just a blip on the screen, not just a problem of a few malformed or malfunctioning priests. There is something that has gone wrong at the very core of the Church's life and self-understanding.

As I read her thoughts, they were suggesting to me that the Body of Christ, which is the Church, has been more concerned with itself, as the body, but not enough as the Body of Christ. I found myself reflecting on this state of spiritual disconnection of the body, form and structure of the Church, from Christ, who

is the source, identity and purpose of the Church, and saw in this state a major cause for abuse of various kinds in the Church, including sexual abuse.

I concur with this assessment, for it corresponds to what I have observed and learned from my multiple dealings with both victims and perpetrators of sexual abuse. More than anything else, it is this complex disconnection that has shocked and angered many in the Church and that poses the greatest demand on trying to define an authentic pastoral care for the people entrusted to me and a credible episcopal ministry in present circumstances.

The challenge, therefore, is to see how to reconnect the body of the Church, with the risen Christ really present in his disciples. This essential connection, which has been lost or forgotten, needs to be rediscovered. The many other actions and responses to sexual abuse, important and necessary as they may be – ensuring best practices and safe environments, returning to more orthodox teaching, or making more robust demands for ethical and moral living – are insufficient to stop deviant sexual behaviour. The central issue in this crisis is not sexual misbehaviour but understanding who we are as Christ's body and what is proper behaviour between and among the many members who make up the Body of Christ.

Based on the principle that action follows being, it is the very nature of how to be Church, here and now, in a relevant and effective manner, that is the real concern and challenge deserving of our attention and commitment. The other actions and whatever else needs to be done will follow and actually make more sense, if we face the real problem. "Seek first the Kingdom of God and all these other things will be given to you as well." (Matthew 6:33) Perhaps we need police, prisons and penitentiaries, given human nature's vulnerabilities and sinfulness, but these have not been very successful in the rehabilitation of deviant behaviour. Fear, constraint and confinement do not positively change a person.

Change only really occurs when the heart is touched. In my years of psychological and human accompaniment of priests, I saw that change occurred when a priest was able to see himself clearly in his strengths and engaged himself totally in the actualization of his strengths. This is not a denial of weakness or vulnerability but a decision to work with what is real, with one's accomplishments, and bring about lasting change. This was always an amazing spiritual transformation. If the priest's heart was not in it, nothing happened, even if he went through the motions. Only the amazing grace of Christ and the priest's restored relationship with Christ could do that.

It is important, therefore, to recover an understanding of the Church as the Body of Christ and not just an institution; to view again the Church as a people where God is the focus, where changed and forgiven brothers and sisters of Christ relate to each other in a healing and healthy way, where they exchange and in-

teract together and care for each other. This is an awareness and an experience of Church that needs to become a lived reality once again if we hope, in our own time, to be relevant and credible again, as a source of hope, joy and light in the world. *Gaudium et Spes* remains the challenge.

Sister Nuala makes the point that at the heart of our being the Church of Christ there must be a change in the manner and depth of how the people of God, priests and laity, interact with each other. This interaction is both a structural issue and a relational one. The people of God, seen and understood as the Body of Christ, suggests a structural set of complex relationships that in present circumstances has become disordered. We know from human experience that when there is something wrong with our bodies, all the parts and structure of the body need to be checked out, to assess where the body's weaknesses are and how these have begun to impede the healthy functioning and the purpose for which the body exists.

If the structure is weakened, can the body be helped? If paralysis is setting in, what can bring new mobility and flexibility to the body? Within the physical body as well as the ecclesiastical one, there are members that can and do malfunction. If we want to make things better, then we need to better understand how the various members and organs relate to each other, what their specific function is, what the optimal conditions are for healthy interaction, and how to bring all the parts of the body to a harmonious and healthier well-being.

This analogy of a well-functioning body, when applied to the Church in our time, helps us to see that there are organic malfunctions within the Church body that require attention. For the body of the Church to function well, it is important to recognize and respect the variety and diversity of all the interrelated members of the body. In the Body of Christ, this would mean allowing the gift and uniqueness of each member to have his or her place, to provide the necessary conditions and context for each member to do only what that member can do well, and to recognize, promote and acknowledge each member's necessary role so that everyone can bring their unique gift to the life of the whole Body of Christ.

All of this, I realize, is not radical new theology. It is as old as the Gospel, but it has been helpful to demonstrate and for me to recognize that in our present circumstances, something from this analogy has been lost. What has gone missing and would be "new for our time" is the capacity and will to acknowledge what the area of malfunction is in order to move on and promote the healing necessary for the Body of Christ to function well again. What has been lost in the life of the Church's functioning is the reality and practice of mutuality.

When the body is well, there is no need to worry about harmony and well-being. It's just there. But when something is wrong, then what ought to be there needs to be worked on. In the present Church, the principle and practice of mutuality so essential to the Church's well-being needs to be rediscovered, promoted and consciously applied. But what is mutuality? It's a relationship of interdependence based upon conscious acceptance and recognition of the value of the other, as other. When mutuality is an operative mindset, it manifests itself in the manner that persons think about others and in the way that persons treat, respect and interact with each other. Mutuality, as a relational disposition, affects and alters the understanding of authority and the way it is exercised; it also changes the way obedience is understood and expressed. More importantly, mutuality impacts the way people collaborate and cooperate with each other. Where the principle of mutuality is operative in an ecclesial context, it colours the episcopal ministry and affects the manner and responsibility of teaching, sanctifying and governing that defines a bishop's apostolic ministry and the pastoral care of the Church entrusted to him and his presbyterate. Lack of, or loss of, mutuality has brought with it disrespect, inadequate assumptions and disordered functioning, giving rise to abuse of authority, of money and of sexuality.

The challenge of Sr. Nuala's analysis is clear. By working on these core matters, abusive behaviour in the Church, whether it is sexual, financial or political, can be diminished. More importantly, the very experience of "Church" as a people who need each other and can count on each other can become a visible new expression for our times of the saying "see how they love one another." (John 13:35) Where mutuality exists, the great commission to go out and proclaim the Gospel gets heard, received and proposed very differently than when the operative relationship in the Church is understood in terms of superior and inferior, when the dynamics of interaction are power-based or when the purpose of the organization is self-perpetuation. For the necessary new age of faith to be inaugurated by the New Evangelization, the Spirit, which gave birth to the Church, must be experienced again. The crisis in which the Church finds herself tells us that we have moved far from a community of faith where the care for each of its members ought to express who we truly are. Instead, these past few years have revealed, by the depth and extent of so much misbehaviour, that in many instances we have become the very opposite of who we are supposed to be.

Perhaps this is why the subject of inadequate understanding of sexuality and the issue of clericalism in the Church recur so often in the diagnostic assessment of the problem of sexual abuse. Inadequate formation and understanding of sexuality and the phenomenon of clericalism are clearly incompatible with the practice and spirit of mutuality. These realities have become obstacles to proper pastoral care and the effective actualization of the Gospel's message. What is more compatible with mutuality is the expression of mercy and the need to offer forgiveness. These person-centred manifestations of mutuality are what provide hope and establish the foundation for knowing the power of the resurrection in daily life. This is what it means to be a Church of redeemed disciples of Christ.

Mutuality between and among the members of the Body of Christ, it seems to me, must be an essential feature in any process that wants to propose and facilitate the personal encounter of Jesus Christ. It is this mutually significant and transforming personal encounter, which occurs only in and through the Body of Christ, that makes the difference to how one lives daily in the Church and how one receives the new and abundant life that Christ provides through the Church. The Church, therefore, needs to recover, in its day-to-day pastoral care, what Christ has to offer and how Christ wants to offer it in order for the Church to be the effective vehicle and sacrament for Christ's healing, guiding, nurturing and reconciling grace.

What Sr. Nuala has pointed out, and I have also come to realize, is that sexual abuse is not just about sex; it is not about what's allowed or not allowed morally, legally, psychologically or emotionally. Sexual abuse is an aberration, and where it exists, it is an expression of a person's disordered state of being, whether or not one sees it this way or understands what that means. That sexual abuse is immoral, illegal, destructive, sinful and still occurs reveals that the perpetrator is not well and has not come to terms sufficiently with his self-understanding as a human sexual being. That so many priests did not see or recognize this and have been unable or unwilling to see sexual abuse as a deviant expression of their sexual identity is very disturbing. That this same phenomenon was unseen or denied by members of the Church, whether in the pews or in positions of leadership, is equally disturbing and indicative of the prevailing and inadequate understanding of sexuality, its force and dynamics, or its proper place in human behaviour. If we are able to see, recognize and acknowledge these inadequacies, as we are doing now, at least it is a sign that we are on the way to getting better. As a bishop and as a Church, I and we can no longer turn away, downplay or deny the multiple issues around psycho-sexual development, the need to address proper ways of experiencing human intimacy, and the importance of developing a more in-depth understanding of the word from Genesis that says "it is not good for man to be alone." (Genesis 2:18)

Sexuality and sexual expression, as a human factor, engages the whole person. As a reality created by God, sexuality is intended to be and can be a balanced, integrated and wholesome experience. In order for it to be so, however, psycho-sexual identity must be in harmony with one's defining and given identity of being male or female. As well, it must not only reflect our culturally conditioned understanding of masculinity and femininity, but must also take into account the kind of man or woman one chooses to be, as this choice must necessarily also include the identifying marks that make us baptized brothers and sisters of Christ, called to serve each other as religious, deacons, priests, bishops and laity. Understanding sexuality, therefore, is not just a biological matter. One must understand its psychological and spiritual components as well. All the elements must be taken into account and integrated. When abuse of a sexual nature is present, all or some of the above components are out of order. Healing becomes a long process of restoring order or discovering it perhaps for the first time. If perfect order is not attainable, and it usually isn't, what can be attained is a grace-supported integral human formation and equilibrium. The balance of body, mind and spirit, in fact, has always been an important and necessary dimension to the experience of being the Church of Christ. Attaining and maintaining such balance has never been easy.

The sexual abuse phenomenon reveals that something is out of balance and has been for many years, particularly in the way some priests saw, understood or imagined themselves in the past and perhaps still do in the present. This is not just a matter of relevance to priests. It involves how some of the laity understood and continue to view priests, as a clerical caste with all kinds of perks and privileges. This special status, and its related sense of entitlement, has sometimes led priests to think of themselves as being above the law, untouchable. The clerical state has too often separated priests from the ordinary experience of daily human living; it has isolated many priests physically and, quite often, psychologically. The idealization of the priest, by self or by others, with inadequate understanding of the depth and dynamics of sexuality, in a mindset where priesthood in practice was about position and function, about power and control, led to the care of souls becoming the destruction of souls. When all these assumptions, practices and culturally based conditions came together, they made for some very volatile and unstable situations, conducive to unhealthy behaviour in more members of the Body of Christ than anyone was ready or able to admit. Now the Church is paying for it! Looking back on these matters, it is not surprising to see that sexual abuse took place. What is scary is that if some of these matters are not attended to, abuse will continue.

These unhealthy conditions did not converge overnight. Sexual abuse is the result of long-standing struggles with the messy human stuff that takes up so much energy in people's lives and occupies so much of the Church's concerns and interest. As a Church we have dealt with sexual abuse from the very beginning of our existence as a community of believers. See St. Paul's first letter to the Corinthians (5:1-3). Unhealthy conditions have been there on and off in every era, giving rise to inadequate ways of behaving and thinking. This is part of the human condition and it highlights why humanity needs a saviour. It's also why the Church exists. After all, the Church is the *Refugium peccatorum*. Recognizing these unhealthy conditions, or not, is what makes the difference between a Church that reflects the Gospel and the mission entrusted to her, or not. When the Church forgets this purpose or raison d'être, we need help and purification.

One of the inadequate ways of behaving and thinking that we struggle with has been clericalism, which is a false understanding of why priests exist. Like any "ism," this particular understanding of clergy brings with it illusions and consequent unacceptable comportment. When certain circumstances converge, combining the unholy spiritual state of being disconnected from Christ, the psychological and emotional state of inadequate self-understanding as a sexual being, the illusions of power and privilege associated with and expected by the clerical state, within a pastoral context of physical and affective isolation, abusive behaviour becomes more than a priority.

The failures of the past, however, must not overwhelm us in the present. We must learn from them. What can we do about all this now? As I struggle along with the present complex realities affecting the Church, I am finding that the sexual abuse problem, as devastating as it is, points to something more serious than sexual abuse by itself. What I see is a Church organization in need of rediscovering itself as a community of faith. There are many faithful disciples of Christ in our Church. Thank God! But we are less an assembly of disciples, less a family of faith, than we ought and need to be. The Spirit of Pentecost needs to be felt again, and a new era of faith must be inaugurated. I hope that Pope Benedict's call for a Year of Faith for 2012–2013 can begin this process.

The Church, for too many, has been reduced to a service centre where people come for whatever it is that one needs at a given time. The Church, in spite of this, is more than a service centre. Priests, as well as bishops, are supposed to be more than attendants and providers of services, or functionaries of the sacred. In the same optic, the faithful are supposed to be more than consumers of religious commodities or goods. The Church is not a religious version of Wal-Mart for cheap grace or a 7-Eleven franchise for spiritual emergencies, nor is Church reducible to the Tim Hortons experience of somewhere to go.

The experience of belonging to a community of faithful brothers and sisters who care for each other, while highly praised and preached, is not the primary experience of Church that prevails in our secular city culture. The reality of God, or the personal encounter of Jesus Christ as Saviour, as Lord, as brother or priest, are not the central defining reference points for many of the baptized in our present Catholic Church. This is why the New Evangelization called for by Pope Benedict is such an amazing challenge for all of us living in Western culture.

For all of the above reasons, something radical needs to be done, and the purification of the Church is a starting point. This process of purification is essentially a spiritual exercise, comparable to the process involved in the First Week of the Spiritual Exercises of St. Ignatius of Loyola. This means seeing and coming to terms with the reality of sin in all its facets and facing the human condition, which requires God's help and salvation. Afterwards, as part of the purification, the healing of mind and heart will come, which results from rediscovering Jesus Christ, grasping again the message of the Gospel, committing oneself with heartfelt faith to the simple yet profound truth that ministry, in all its expressions, ordained or not, is about caring for each other with the respect due to each other, for no other reason than because we are all baptized followers of Christ and, as such, we must do for others what Christ does for us.

What I have described as purification is a first step that goes hand in hand with the amazing vision for a New Evangelization. The New Evangelization is what presently engages most of my energy and episcopal ministry. Through the implementation of this call and challenge, I hope to make some kind of impact on the Church entrusted to my care. I pray that with a rediscovery of the power of the Holy Spirit and lots of help from those interested, some kind of healing will occur not only with regards to sexual abuse, but, more importantly, for all vulnerable areas in the body of the Body of Christ. The prescriptions for the presently ailing body that is the Church are not simple. There is no magic pill or rule or practice that will solve all our problems or restore us to health. What is needed to improve the situation is the collaboration of people of faith, a balanced combination of all the available human remedies along with a spirit renewed by a push from the Holy Spirit.

In keeping with the diagnostic reflection of Sister Nuala's book, I recall participating some years ago in a multi-disciplinary diagnostic conference, in a hospital setting, where I was the chaplain at the time. That experience taught me that every patient is a complex organism and a human being. I was asked by the lead doctor to participate in the conference because he said to me, "You have a different understanding of the patient before us. You see the person, whereas most of the professionals see the problem, which is the particular specialty of interest to each of them. It's important that you be there so we don't forget that we are dealing with a person."

This recollection of a long-ago memory helps me to see and not forget that the Church is like that person. The Church is complex, multi-faceted, and each area of Church life can become the focus of one's specialized attention, sometimes overly so! But we must not let the symptom become the problem, nor must we let the problem overtake the person. In the pastoral care of the Church, it's the Person of Christ whom we must keep in mind and try to better understand and to model. Just as Christ never treated people as problems but as persons, so, too, we must stay focused on the person of Jesus Christ and not just on the problems affecting the members of the Body of Christ. We do this by reconnecting with Christ, by rediscovering our love for him and our gratitude for his self-sacrifice. It is the person of Christ who transforms us. It is up to us to appreciate his ministry, receive his forgiveness and accept his mercy. This will allow us to experience the power of the resurrection, and nothing will ever be the same.

† *Anthony Mancini*
Archbishop of Halifax-Yarmouth

PERSONAL PREFACE

MY JOURNEY: FROM DIAGNOSING CHILDREN TO DIAGNOSING SINS AGAINST CHILDREN

"… we cannot keep from speaking about what we have seen and heard"
(Acts 4:20)

They are afraid of offending and making enemies – and all of this because of self-love. Sometimes, it's just that they would like to keep peace, and this, I tell you, is the worst cruelty one can inflict. If a sore is not cauterized or excised when necessary, but only ointment is applied, not only will it not heal, but it will infect the whole body, often fatally.—Catherine of Siena, Doctor of the Church, from a letter to Pope Gregory XI[1]

There are days when I cringe at the thought of working on the issue of clergy sexual abuse. I don't want to see another headline. I don't want to explain to yet another friend or colleague why I am still a Catholic – and a nun at that! I am tired of being embarrassed by, and angry with, the Church in whose service I've given my life. I turn regularly to Jesus at Gethsemane, pleading, "Father, if it be possible, let this cup pass." Yet I feel an undeniable call to work in this area, even while others around me seem to sleep comfortably in denial or have "moved on" or moved out of the Church.

We may all be tired of allegations and suits and criminal charges. We may be angry, negative or cynical and express our feelings in disrespectful chatter about this crisis, but we have not yet entered into real conversation about what this crisis says about how we are as a Church. We need to begin a deeper discussion and reflection on where the Spirit is calling us now.

Like Peter and John in the Acts of the Apostles, I cannot keep from speaking about what I have seen and heard of this crisis and its importance for the Church. Dealing with this issue has led me to places I did not want to go, and to knowledge I did not want to have, and even to say things it would be more comfortable not to speak. But "By the grace of God I am what I am." (1 Corinthians 15:10) I bear a burden of responsibility here that is intimately caught up in the grace of my vocation and my history with the early work of the Canadian Church on clergy sexual abuse.

I entered religious life in September 1962, just as the Second Vatican Council opened. My entire religious formation was under the influence of the halcyon days of that Council. The vision was that of the Church as the People of God, a priestly people, where the gifts of all were needed and where the celebration of the Eucharist required the active participation of all, to thank the Lord for gifts and graces and be strengthened for the ministry of all in proclaiming the Good News. In that strange and wonderful set of contradictions and graces called vocation, I was chosen by my Congregation for higher studies and given permission to study medicine at Dalhousie University in Halifax, Nova Scotia, as the first religious sister to attend its medical school. I received an MD in 1972 and completed paediatric specialty training in Halifax and in Boston, Massachusetts, in 1975.

Caring for sick and dying children has been a great grace in my life. I have been privileged to experience some of the strength and courage of children as well as their extreme vulnerability and dependence on adults for care and protection. "By the grace of God I am what I am …" a woman with a strong sense of baptismal vocation; a member of a religious community founded by St. Elizabeth Ann Seton, whose dying words were "Be children of the Church"; a child of the Second Vatican Council; and a paediatrician.

The Early Work on Clergy Sexual Abuse

In May 1989, in the wake of devastating revelations about sexual abuse in the Irish Christian Brothers' Mount Cashel Orphanage and subsequent accusations against six priests and two former priests of the Archdiocese of St. John's, Newfoundland, Archbishop Alphonsus Penney took a courageous and unprecedented step in creating a Special Archdiocesan Commission of Enquiry into the Sexual Abuse of Children by Members of the Clergy in St. John's [Newfoundland]. The Commission's mandate was to identify *what* had happened and, even more crucially, *why* it had happened. As a woman religious and the newly minted Professor of Paediatrics at Dalhousie University and Chief of Paediatrics at the Izaak Walton Killam Hospital for Children in Halifax, I was asked to participate.

As a general paediatrician, I had experience of the horrors of child physical and sexual abuse. Clergy sexual abuse was *terra incognita*. I had no experience of this uncharted land of abuse in the Church, and I was unaware that navigating the spiritual and ecclesial hills, valleys, crevices and dark forests was going to be so difficult. Five Commissioners, led by the former Lieutenant Governor of Newfoundland and devout Anglican layman Gordon Winter, entered into this pain-filled land in faith and hope. We had little understanding of the courage and uniqueness of what we were about. We soon came to understand why ancient mapmakers would add "There be dragons here" to *terra incognita*. Dragons and demons indeed!

We were unprepared for the depth and breadth of the devastation to Catholic Newfoundland. We decided to enter this territory in two ways: first we reviewed the empirical and scholarly literature on sexual abuse of children and youth, and then we opened ourselves to the actual experience of the Church of Newfoundland via public engagement. The Commission created a bibliography of what was known in 1990. Of the slightly more than one hundred references on child sexual abuse, fewer than half a dozen were explicitly on clergy sexual abuse of children.

Because secrecy and denial characterized the history of this problem, we made a conscious decision to listen to the pain and suffering of those affected. We held public meetings in St. John's and in the parishes that had been most directly affected. We tried to listen carefully and hear the pain of victims, their families and friends, parishes and the remaining active priests of the Archdiocese.

Two images are indelibly impressed on my mind and heart. The first is an elderly weather-worn gentleman, clearly a man of the sea and uncomfortable with speaking in public, who rose to his feet and with tears streaming down his face, told us of the abuse of a beloved nephew at the hands of Fr. James Hickey, who was then incarcerated at Dorchester Penitentiary. The man's pain and anger were palpable, but so, too, was his desolation as he cried out, "I haven't been able to talk to my God since I heard of this, and I don't think I ever will again." My heart was broken at the thought that he could not go to the Lord at the time he needed his healing and consolation most. I had witnessed the devastation of child sexual abuse by fathers, uncles, family friends and sport coaches. This abuse by a priest was all that and something far more. As a woman of faith who loved the Church and had committed her life to a ministry of continuing the healing and reconciling mission of Jesus, this betrayal was almost more than I could bear.

The second image that haunts me is from the meeting the Commission held with the remaining active priests of the Archdiocese. Four priests and two for-

15

mer members of the clergy were under investigation and had been relieved from ministry. Two priests were in jail at the time. I find it difficult to describe what it was like to look out at the assembled priests. I remember thinking that I had never seen such a sad and confused group of men in my life. They appeared shell-shocked. Their lives and ministry had been changed forever by the actions of fellow priests. Having heard repeatedly of priests being "on a pedestal" as a factor in the abuse, I saw men in the depths. If they had been on pedestals, these were lonesome and risky places indeed!

The grace of the Newfoundland work was twofold. First, it was rooted in both empirical and scientific data and in the experience of Newfoundlanders. Second, in identifying *why* the abuse happened as it did, the Commission rejected simple answers and concluded that "… no single cause can account for the sexual abuse … rather, it is the Commission's view that a combination of factors coincided to allow the abuse to occur."[2]

The Commission then identified six themes around these factors that needed to be prayerfully and honestly explored in order for healing to occur and prevention to be effective: "power, education, sexuality, support of priests, management, and avoidance of scandal." This crisis is not just about individual sins and crimes; it goes deeper. This crucial identification of the importance of these deep systemic and cultural factors is recognized, even today, in history,

> … when the Archdiocese of St. John's Newfoundland published its groundbreaking *Report of the Archdiocesan Commission of Enquiry into the Sexual Abuse of Children by Members of the Clergy*, the initial assumption that these occurrences were rare and isolated could no longer be sustained.[3]

I also participated in the Canadian Conference of Catholic Bishops' (CCCB) Ad Hoc Committee on Child Sexual Abuse which, in 1992, produced *From Pain to Hope*,[4] a resource focusing on protocols, screening for entrance to the seminary and seminary education, and *Breach of Trust, Breach of Faith*,[5] a discussion guide for parishes and lay groups to foster a culture of openness in pursuing the underlying factors. In Canada, *From Pain to Hope* made an impact in many, but not all, dioceses. *Breach of Trust, Breach of Faith* was used rarely; in some dioceses it was not used at all. Twenty years ago, most clergy and laity believed that talking about this issue would just make it worse or were unprepared for dialogue.

I believed that I had contributed to some important, though personally difficult, work for the Church. I assumed there would be follow-up research and reflection on these underlying themes and I moved on. When I am wrong I am really wrong!

Unfinished Business

I was more angered than anything else by the 2002 revelations of clergy sexual abuse in the Archdiocese of Boston. It was the Newfoundland experience all over again, but on a much larger scale. I was appalled at the ignorance of the Newfoundland work published ten full years before. It appeared that nothing had really been learned from the pain and suffering of the Newfoundland Church or the many other works, reports and court cases in the ten years since. Similarities between Newfoundland and Boston in denial, minimization of harm and preferential protection of the priest-offender and Church reputation, rather than the needs of the victim-survivors, confirmed for me that the systemic and cultural factors at work in fostering the abuse and negligent mismanagement transcended geography and local culture.

But I was not knocked off my horse in St. Paul style until September 2009, with the arrest of Bishop Raymond Lahey for possession and importation into Canada of child pornography, a month after he had negotiated a major settlement for victims of clergy abuse in his diocese of Antigonish, Nova Scotia. My world changed that day because Lahey had been a priest in St. John's at the time of the Newfoundland Commission. The news, coming over the car radio, shocked me to my core. I had to pull over to the side of the road as I had an unprecedented experience of flashback to Newfoundland. I could see again the tearful uncle who had lost faith and trust in God over the betrayal by a priest. I could feel again my own pain and anger. I thought I was going to be physically sick. If I had been on a horse, I would certainly have fallen off.

Just as Paul had "scales fall from his eyes" (Acts 9:18) after his experience, I had a painfully sharp and vividly clear insight that we had not finished the work of Newfoundland. We had increased awareness of the issue in society and in the Church, and had influenced improvements in seminary screening and preparation and in protocols for responsible ministry. But, in medical terms, I saw all this as a kind of symptomatic relief; important work, but not getting to the core of the problem. We had not pursued the underlying systemic and cultural factors, which allowed all this to happen. Our failure to address *why* this crisis has occurred as it has in our Church has compounded the pain and suffering. Nearly twenty-five years after that question of *why* was first asked, we have still not come to clear and compelling answers. No wonder healing is elusive.

My recommitment to this issue began with an appeal to the CCCB at its October 2010 Plenary Conference to take up the "unfinished business" of the early 1990s and once again provide leadership into these deeper systemic and cultural issues. With the collaboration of a colleague from McGill University's Centre for Research on Religion, Professor Daniel Cere, and support from a number of sources, including the CCCB, I organized a conference in Montreal in October 2011.[6] It focused on the lessons learned from this experience and the challenges for the Church. This experience confirmed for me that there is a hunger to speak of this openly in order to respond to the spiritual conversion and transformation to which this crisis calls us.

I am blessed that my own bishop, Anthony Mancini of Halifax-Yarmouth, who assumed interim administration for the Diocese of Antigonish in the wake of Bishop Lahey's resignation, is empathetically aware of the magnitude of harm done and understands the depths of the spiritual and ecclesial crisis. In his "Letter to all Catholics in Nova Scotia" following Bishop Lahey's arrest, Archbishop Mancini wrote:

> Enough is enough! How much more can all of us take? Like you, my heart is broken, my mind is confused, my body hurts and I have moved in and out of a variety of feelings, especially shame and frustration, fear and disappointment, along with a sense of vulnerability, and a tremendous poverty of spirit. I have cried and I have silently screamed, and perhaps that was my prayer to God: Why Lord? What does all this mean? What are you asking of me and my priests? What do you want to see happen among your people? Is this a time of purification or is it nothing more than devastation? Are people going to stop believing, will faithful people stop being people of faith? Lord, what are you asking of us and how can we make it happen?[7]

I am convinced it is a time of healing and purification. We can make that happen only by being open to the Spirit; only if we "Let the same mind be in you that was in Christ Jesus." (Philippians 2:5)

Pope Benedict XVI has called for this deeper analysis and understanding, also using the metaphor of diagnosis: "Only by examining carefully the many elements that gave rise to the present crisis can a clear-sighted diagnosis of its causes be undertaken and effective remedies be found."[8]

As a physician, I agree completely with the Holy Father that appropriate and effective treatment requires a clear-sighted diagnosis. Individual victim-survivors suffer; the whole Body of Christ suffers. We can no longer deny that we are in crisis. A crisis is a turning point; in a medical crisis, life and death are on the line. We recognize these times when we hear "the fever has broken," "we removed the whole tumour," and "she has awakened from the coma." It is this kind of life- and holiness-threatening crisis that we are experiencing in the Church. Healing can occur, but only if we have the faith, hope and courage to come together to acknowledge our need and to reflect together on how to respond to the Lord's question.

While writing this book has been an intensely solitary and often painful experience, it could not have been done without the support of many others. Special thanks is due to my Community, the Sisters of Charity of Halifax, for supporting me through this work; to Tim Krahn, my tireless research assistant; to Archbishop Emeritus James M. Hayes; to the many who graciously read early versions, especially Sister Donna Brady SSM and the Gather the Wisdom Group, Delmar Wagner, James Roche, Fr. William Hann and Archbishop Anthony Mancini.

"Lord, save us! We are perishing!" And Jesus said to them, "Why are you afraid, you of little faith?" (Matthew 8:25-26)

Sr. Nuala Kenny
Halifax, Nova Scotia
May 31, 2012

INTRODUCTION

Jesus said, "Those who are well have no need of a physician, but those who are sick." (Matthew 9:12)

This latest crisis is an opportunity to discover Jesus even closer to us than we had imagined. It is a crisis caused by our own failures as a Church, but God can make it a blessing, if we live it in faith.—Timothy Radcliffe, OP[1]

The sexual abuse of children and youth by Roman Catholic clergy is the most significant crisis in the history of the modern Church. Virtually no diocese in North America has been unscathed by the resulting scandal, massive diversion of resources to settlements, and time spent by bishops and other senior Church officials on it.

Between 1950 and 2010 there were 16,000 reported victims in the United States alone.[2] Because of general under-reporting of the problem, which has been identified again and again when criminal inquiries and civil litigation become involved, the number is much higher. US bishops have reported approximately 6,000 allegations against clergy in this same timeline, resulting in an incidence of 5.4 percent of active priests. Under-reporting and assessments from jurisdictions where there has been intense scrutiny, such as Los Angeles, Boston and Philadelphia, make the real number closer to 10,000 priests. Nineteen bishops have been accused. In the US, between 1984 and 2009 there were over 3,000 lawsuits; settlements are over three billion dollars.[3] Bankruptcy has been declared by at least eight US dioceses, as well as by the Oregon province of the Jesuits and the Irish Christian Brothers.

Canada has not maintained central records, but the issues and responses are similar[4] and the numbers would be proportional, adding thousands of victims and hundreds of clergy offenders to the North American total. Ireland has been devastated by this crisis.[5] Europe and Australia have also been impacted; we are seeing data emerging from there.

Today, there is a large and growing literature on the issue of sexual abuse in the Catholic Church from a wide variety of solid sources. We have commission reports, empirical research, clinical narratives, survivor memoirs, court cases, grand jury judgments, and theoretical work in theology, sociology, psychology and criminology. This literature provides insight into a wide range of systemic and cultural factors at work here and is invaluable at getting to the deeper diagnosis. But Church leadership is focused on prevention of individual cases through screening for seminary entrance along with improved seminary formation, policies for safe ministry environments, and protocols for managing allegations.

All of this has been occurring in a time of decline of religion in society, shifts in Church attendance, changing demographics within practising Catholics, and loss of priestly vocations in the Church, especially in North America.

In any other organization, such chaos and devastation would be recognized as a tipping point resulting in either dissolution or substantive reform and renewal. In theological and spiritual terms, it would be a time for repentance, purification and transformation. There have been many different responses from both clergy and laity: some continue to deny the scope of the tragedy or see it as a vast conspiracy against the Church; some accept that bad things were perpetrated by sick or sinful individuals but try to carry on with their personal spiritual lives; some cope by making elaborate distinctions between the Church as the People of God and the hierarchical Church; others have experienced these revelations as the last straw and, in anger or despair or disgust, have left the Church. Church leadership has overwhelmingly responded with specific preventive measures, such as protocols for dealing with allegations and policies for reporting and creating safe ministry environments.

There are some who have raised their voices for deep purification and renewal. They demonstrate that this is a time for that prophetic criticism and prophetic energizing that is linked to hope. The biblical scholar Walter Brueggemann reminds us that "real criticism begins in the capacity to grieve …."[6] Prophetic criticism is about anguish, not anger.[7] The abuse crisis has caused all who reflect prayerfully on these actions and events to mourn the loss of belief and trust in the Church as a place of holiness and justice – a sacrament of salvation and a community of love.

Prophets break with triumphalism and oppression and move us to the freedom of God and to ways of justice and compassion. But they need to overcome passivity and denial and the numbness that many experience when clergy abuse is mentioned. The Jewish theologian Abraham Heschel has said,

The more deeply immersed I became in the thinking of the prophets, the more powerfully it became clear to me what the lives of the prophets sought to convey: that morally speaking, there is no limit to the concern one must feel for the suffering of human beings, that indifference to evil is worse than evil itself, that in a free society, some are guilty, but all are responsible.[8]

All in the Church have a responsibility to respond to this crisis; all must participate in the healing of the individual victim-survivors and of the Church itself.

Brueggemann posits that the community that can generate prophecy needs at least four things:
- a long and available memory,
- a sense of pain and loss,
- the active practice of hope,
- an effective mode of discourse.[9]

Have we the capacity to generate prophecy here? The Church certainly has a long memory of its grace-filled and sinful history. The sense of pain and loss is palpable and enduring. The active practice of hope, a belief that "nothing will be impossible with God" (Luke 1:37) is being tested in this crisis. Fostering effective discourse is the particular object of this work.

As a paediatrician, I know well that denial is a natural human reaction in the face of unbearable pain and suffering. Some denial early on in a diagnosis can be important for coping with bad news. But persistent denial, in the face of ongoing, unrelieved pain and suffering, becomes at least as pathological as the underlying condition. I fail to understand why we are all not shaken to the bone by what we now know of this crisis in our Church. This is not just a crisis for "them" – clergy-abusers and bishop-managers. This is a crisis for all who are the Church. Church leadership seems fixed on the sins and crimes of individual men – priest offenders, bishops who mismanaged – and policies and protocols. Important as all that is, it is not enough. The call here is first and foremost for purification and spiritual conversion. Only a change of heart rightly changes structures and practices. Only conversion to the mind and heart of Jesus will help us discover which structures and practices have facilitated this crisis and which will foster a healthy and holy Church.

For many bishops, priests and laity, there is a fear that attempts to discuss the *why* of the abuse crisis will make things worse; others fear that the issues many want to blame for the crisis – mandatory celibacy, all-male clergy, lack of female priests, and homosexuality – raise foundational moral and theological issues, which cannot be dealt with by any single diocese or bishop, or even by a national Church. So, for them, to enter into any open and truthful dialogue about concerns is to raise unrealistic expectation. The exercise is doomed.

While a diagnosis of cultural and systemic factors will raise questions about structures and practices, the primary causes will clearly be of heart and mind in contradiction to the mind of Christ. Many bishops know this is a deeper crisis, but appear afraid to take it on because of fear of making diagnoses different from those of the Vatican or diagnoses that call for fundamental changes in the way we are as Church.

The crisis calls for purification, transformation and renewal. Its effect is bigger and deeper than any of the prevailing and damaging liberal–conservative divisions in the Church today. There are widely differing understandings of the nature of the crisis; these understandings map closely to different views of what it is to be authentically Catholic in the post-Christendom world. In St. Paul's words, "I appeal to you, brothers and sisters … that all of you be in agreement and that there be no divisions among you, but that you be united in the same mind and the same purpose." (1 Corinthians 1:10)

Pope Benedict XVI has called for a New Evangelization in the West. Such a call for recommitment to following Christ in the modern post-Christendom world is timely. However, we need to renew from within before we can be authentic and trustworthy witnesses of the loving, merciful and reconciling Christ to our world. All attempts will fail if they do not take account of this crisis and what it has revealed about the state of health and holiness of the Church, understood here as the Body of Christ.

This modest work is a tool intended to promote and facilitate open, honest and prayerful dialogue among Catholics about clergy sexual abuse in our Church. It is aimed at breaking the culture of silence and denial that has characterized the crisis itself. While there is much talk in informal circles about the abuse in the Church, virtually all of it is negative, ill-informed and discouraged because there is no clear way forward. This work is in a prayerful reflection–dialogue–workbook format precisely because we must all participate in finding the way forward, and we must do it intentionally, focused on the Lord Jesus and who he has called us to be.

So this work is a tool to promote prayerful and effective discourse in this complex and difficult area. It has been written with attention to some key principles of adult learning:

- The issue must be relevant to the learner; they need or want to know.
- The process of learning engages the emotions.
- The experience of all participants is crucially important.
- The learning ought to have a practical outcome.[10]

These principles are very different from the usual mode of discourse in the Church, which is passive receipt of information from authorities. It will take practice and patience and prayer.

Using the metaphor of diagnosis, we will explore an accurate diagnosis of the present state of the Body of Christ resulting from the clergy abuse crisis and identify some elements in any effective prescription for healing the Church. This book and its reflection–discussion format is meant to assist us in understanding what is known about this crisis, to prayerfully reflect on it, to respectfully and openly share our experiences and insights, and to help us together to identify some of the way forward. As a result, this book is structured so that each chapter provides a referenced summary of the important issues and information, a sharing of relevant Gospel images and words, and a set of initial questions for reflection and action. These reflection questions are designed to be used by individuals or groups after the material is read and some time has been spent in calling to mind Gospel passages that speak of an alternative vision or way of acting. Ideally, this is a communal exercise that would include ordained and lay, priest and people together trying to discern where the Spirit is calling us.

In Chapter 1, we focus on understanding the pain and suffering of the individual victims, especially the spiritual consequences of abuse by clergy; review the disturbing dynamics of sexual abuse by clergy; and consider profiles of abusing clergy.

Chapter 2 outlines some of the history of the sexual abuse of children and youth by Roman Catholic clergy and religious; analyzes the now well-documented and disturbingly consistent pattern of response by Church leaders across national cultures – denial, secrecy ("don't talk about it"), and protection of priest abusers and institutional reputation over the needs of vulnerable victims; and identifies some important characteristics of the priest offenders.

In Chapter 3 we assess some diagnoses offered to date and their proposed treatments, including apologies, screening of candidates for ordination, improved human and sexual formation of priests, protocols for responsible ministry, and financial restitution to victim-survivors; and identify the importance of more in-depth analysis of the cultural and systemic factors that fostered the shape and scope of the crisis.

Chapter 4 situates sexual abuse as fundamentally an abuse of power. We reflect on relationships and power in the Church and identify clericalism, a distorted understanding of the role and function of bishops and priests with profound implications for the laity, as the particular form of abuse of power that has facilitated the ongoing crisis in the Church.

We give our attention to the complex and compelling area of human sexuality in Chapter 5. We review the Catholic experience of sexuality with its secrecy and negativity regarding human sexuality, moral theology with its sin-centred approach, and an inadequate theology of sexuality, for their possible roles in this crisis.

Chapter 6 moves us into summarizing what we have learned and addressing healing. We distinguish treatment of individual acts of clergy sexual abuse of children and youth from the treatment of the broader and ongoing crisis of management. Diagnosing this crisis as, first and foremost, a spiritual and ecclesial one, we identify some crucial elements in any prescription: acknowledgement of the call to all of purification and renewal, and reclamation of the priesthood of the baptized and the Eucharistic community, where the gifts of all are accepted as necessary. Healing requires an acceptance that mutuality is central, "since pastors and the other faithful are bound to each other by a mutual need."[11]

We close with some thoughts on prognosis. Is the outcome a return to full health and holiness, or to a chronic illness, or to death? While we believe in the power of the Holy Spirit, the Church is a divinely instituted but thoroughly human institution. The prognosis is guarded precisely because of our ongoing denial of the severity of the situation and our human resistance to change. We have varying degrees of willingness to be truly purified and renewed, and our readiness to change is related to the present condition of the Church, with some of us hurting, others in denial, and some of us simply walking away.

"Lord, to whom can we go?" (John 6:68)

CHAPTER 1

THE PAIN AND SUFFERING OF CLERGY SEXUAL ABUSE

"If any of you put a stumbling block before one of these little ones who believe in me, it would be better for you if a great millstone were fastened around your neck and you were drowned in the depth of the sea." (Matthew 18:6)

Sexual abuse by some clergy and religious has caused great suffering and spiritual harm to victims. It has been damaging in the life of the Church ... Sexual abuse within the Church is a profound contradiction of the teaching and witness of Christ.—Pope John Paul II[1]

The healing of our bodies, minds and souls requires an accurate diagnosis of our state of ill health, an appropriate prescription, a compliant patient, and more than a little grace. All diagnosis begins with the experience of one who suffers. It is no different for victim-survivors of clergy sexual abuse of children and youth and, indeed, the whole Body of Christ. We need to try to understand the full range of pain and suffering resulting from this crisis: first and foremost for the victim-survivors, and then for the whole Church.

Just as a doctor pursues details of the pain, suffering or dysfunction that bring a patient to medical attention, so we must understand accurately and in some detail the pain, suffering and dysfunction from sexual abuse of children and youth. If this were the common cold or minor trauma, the diagnosis would be easy. Prescriptions could be provided without much attention to the details of what happened or further investigation. But the ill health of the Church – whether we describe it as pain, trauma, a cancer consuming from within, or an infection eroding from without – is a major threat to the health and holiness of the Church.

Serious conditions require serious work in diagnosis and careful, considered attention to the patient's symptoms.

We know from personal medical encounters that this questioning can be time-consuming, annoying and even humiliating, as we are asked to reveal intimate details of our body functions. While talk shows and family gatherings demonstrate that some of us revel in talking about the most intimate details of our medical conditions, the vast majority of us are far more embarrassed and reluctant. Some of us deny completely our need for medical attention. This denial is especially true for men.

We need to begin our reflections, then, with focused attention on pain and suffering. In the usual medical encounter, the patient is clearly identified. However, the clergy abuse crisis has harmed many people. There are two separate but related pathologies at work here:

- first and foremost is the pain and suffering of the individual victim-survivors emanating directly from their abuse as children and youth by Roman Catholic clergy and from the responses to their revelations of abuse;
- then there is the pain and suffering for the whole Church, the Body of Christ, resulting from the management of the abuse of individuals. To say this is not to minimize the harm to victim-survivors, but to acknowledge the full range of devastation of this issue.

In this chapter we start our reflections by attending to the immediate and direct pain and suffering of victim-survivors of sexual abuse by clergy.

Objectives

In this first reflection we will

1. try to comprehend some of the pain and suffering resulting from sexual abuse of children and youth by clergy, with special attention to their spiritual suffering;
2. explore the central dynamics of sexual abuse of children and youth by clergy;
3. share some Gospel images of a prophetic alternative; and
4. propose some initial questions for reflection and discussion.

1. The Pain and Suffering of Sexual Abuse of Children and Youth by Clergy

We now have many sources of information about the sexual abuse of children and youth by clergy of all religious denominations and its devastating effects. The information comes from reports, commissions, scientific studies, judicial inquiries, court documents and theological analysis. There is also a wealth of heart-rending information available in the personal narratives of some victim-survivors. The literature is clear about staggering numbers and abuse of a very serious nature. It is a story of real horror. Many of these resources focus on abuse of children and youth by members of the Roman Catholic clergy.[2] The Roman Catholic Church has become a particular object of attention for a number of reasons, not the least of which is the number of high-profile cases.[3]

We may want to avoid the lurid details of what actually happened. But denial and secrecy are central to this issue. Unless and until we confront the evil and harm here, we will not be able to address it. It is essential that we try to develop some empathic understanding of the traumatic experiences, pain and anger of victim-survivors, even as the learning causes us pain, anger, disgust and a possible crisis of faith. The physical, emotional and spiritual suffering of victim-survivors has been great.

It is profoundly disturbing to think about boys and girls being seduced with fear and threats or with alcohol, drugs and pornographic films and then groped, sodomized and raped. It is almost unbearable to know that the perpetrators were men of God. But this is what has happened. We have to try and understand their experiences with our heads, hearts and faith. We have to see these brothers and sisters in Christ as they were when they were harmed – young and vulnerable. And, as I mentioned in the Introduction, there are many victim-survivors to see and hear.

There was a wide range of abuse, some of it so sickening, degrading, blasphemous and sacrilegious that even trying to recount it is painful. For some who dismiss what happened as "just fondling," the record is clear that "most of the abuse reported was of a very serious nature and occurred numerous times; roughly half of accused priests were known or suspected to have had more than one victim and 80% of victims were male …."[4] It is difficult to know how explicit to be about the abuse so that those who deny or minimize the harm can possibly gain insight and those who are sensitive to the issue are not so disgusted they can't participate in reflection and discussion.

Here, in the simplest language and without any graphic depiction of the horrific acts, we will reflect on a very typical case. This case is repeated again and again in reports, court cases and first-person accounts.

JOHN'S STORY

In 1970, John is a normal 12-year-old boy from a devout Catholic family. Fr. X, newly assigned to John's parish, is enthusiastic and charismatic. He rapidly focuses his ministry on children and youth, with particular attention to boys between 10 and 14 years of age. The priest is soon involved with many activities, from sports to altar boys and summer camps.

The priest develops a particularly close relationship with John, who comes from a stable home with high Church involvement. Fr. X is a welcome guest in John's home. The family thinks nothing of sending John up to the rectory at all times to help out Fr. X. The family is happy and honoured that their boy is special to Father. John has been taught to honour the priest as the representative of Christ himself. John's trust and that of his entire family in this man of God was high.

One morning sex is introduced. After John serves Mass, Fr. X helps John remove his alb and suddenly presses himself against the boy and starts to rub himself against him. John is stunned into silence. A pattern develops. The acts escalate from fondling to oral sex and rape. Fr. X explains that what he is doing is a holy thing because he is a holy man, and John is sworn to keep this special secret between them. The abuse occurs in the rectory, in the sacristy and at the diocesan summer camp. John is shocked, confused and physically hurt. He feels that the abuse is his fault because he has in some way tempted this holy man! The same man who presides over Sunday Mass and is honoured by his family and community does these terrible things to him.

As John becomes more uncomfortable with what is happening, Fr. X threatens him and his family with eternal damnation if John tells. Finally, John reveals to his parents what is happening, and they are shocked. At first they do not believe him and John is further victimized. Then they come to understand this is all true. They go to their pastor, who says he is certain John has misunderstood Fr. X, but assures them he will take care of this. They are cautioned not to speak about the issue for fear of bringing scandal to the Church. John's parents trust that it would be taken care of.

Fr. X is called in and reprimanded; he promises not to do it again, and he is then moved to a new parish, which is given no information about his recent behaviour. John's parents are relieved to see him go. John's experience is repeated again and again with other boys in the new parish.

Neither John nor his family is given support or counselling. Today, in his 50s, John looks back on a life of emotional and spiritual chaos.

As there are thousands of known victim-survivors and thousands of clergy offenders, some variance is found among individual cases, but John's story captures the common elements of abuse by clergy and religious. Many victims were from homes with disruption and discord, where the victims were particularly vulnerable to attention from an adult male. Many victim-survivors have never disclosed the abuse. Some of them disclosed it and were not believed. Many offending clergy were not slick and charismatic, but isolated and socially immature.

By the mid-1980s, new elements were added to the story. Some victim-survivors, now adults, spoke up and were heard, and the Church sometimes paid for their counselling. The offending priest was likely sent for treatment before being reassigned. But treatment effectiveness became unclear and contested. Reassignment was most often to another parish, which was not informed of the priest's history of abuse, and his unsupervised access to children and youth resumed. By the mid-1990s, there was another twist in the story. Victim-survivors, now 20 and 30 years after the abuse, and frustrated by the internal Church response, initiated legal actions. These suits and settlements gave some victim-survivors a sense of control or payback and resources for counselling.

John's story is important in that its elements mirror situations as different as that of Fr. Gilbert Gauthe's in Henry, Louisiana, the first publicized case in North America in 1983, and Fr. James Hickey's, the highly publicized 1989 case from St. John's, Newfoundland. John's story also mirrors the 2002 revelations against Fr. John Geoghan in Boston. Newfoundland, Louisiana and Boston could hardly be more different culturally, but the stories of priestly abuse could hardly be more similar.

For some within the Church, skepticism about the real and enduring harm of the sexual abuse of children and youth still exists. Some Catholics even blame older children and youth for participating in incidents of abuse and not disclosing them. These Catholics fail to understand the complexity of sexual abuse and how much secrecy and control are central. Society has no such skepticism. In May 2011, Amnesty International named the Vatican on human rights concerns for not sufficiently complying with international mandates, to which it is a signatory, protecting children from abuse. This is serious criticism for a Church where protection of life, especially of the most vulnerable, is a central belief, and it should rock us all to our core. Skepticism is simply inexcusable in light of the facts.

Today, there is a wealth of information on the painful consequences of sexual abuse; most of it devastating and lifelong without treatment.[5] Some victims have no apparent long-term consequences. They are the exceptions and seem to be people whose experiences were limited and who did not have a close relationship with the offender. Victims of early sexual violation cannot reconcile the trusted person – father, uncle, coach or parish priest – with the sexually over-stimulating man who abuses them. There is an irretrievable loss of childhood and its sense of safety and trust in others. The victims frequently develop a post-traumatic stress disorder that can affect all areas of life and can last for years after the abuse has stopped. For many sufferers, an evocative encounter – the scent of incense, sun streaming through a stained-glass window, and so on – is enough to send them into panicky flashbacks. There are a number of long-standing consequences, including dissociation and unexpected regression to their victimized selves; identification with the greedy and insatiable offender; difficulties with interpersonal relations and trust; problems with normal sexual activity; and interference with cognitive function in interpersonal situations.[6] Suicide is not an uncommon event among victim-survivors.

In addition to the general consequences of sexual abuse, the sexual exploitation of children and youth by members of the clergy has direct and serious consequences to faith and spirituality.[7] We need to appreciate the depth of harm, particularly spiritual harm, to victims of sexual abuse when the perpetrator is a "man of God," an "alter *Christus*." The title "Slayer of the soul," taken from a poem written by a priest-abuser in one of the first books on the issue, conveys some sense of the depth of spiritual devastation.[8]

There is a powerful emerging genre of testimonial by survivors of clergy sexual abuse that helps us comprehend the effects on individual lives.[9] These heart-rending stories tell of the effects of abuse on their emotional and psychological well-being, but also on their understanding of God and the holy, the sacraments and the priestly. Because the priest represents God, to be violated by a priest is to feel violated and abandoned by God. The stories tell of victims who prayed fervently for the abuse to stop, but God did not answer their prayers. The faith of these children was deliberately assaulted, exploited, abused and often mortally wounded. This assault on faith was exacerbated when Church officials were seen to tolerate the abusive behaviour and protect the offender over the victim. Fundamental notions of the right and good and holy were perverted. Cardinal Marc Ouellet, Prefect for the Congregation of Bishops, in his homily at a Penitential Vigil in association with the February 2012 Vatican Symposium "Towards Healing and Renewal," acknowledged the devastation this way: "Abuse is a crime, in fact, which causes an authentic experience of death for the innocent victims, whom God alone can truly raise to new life in the person of the Holy Spirit."[10]

The Church has not yet addressed adequately the spiritual losses from sexual abuse by clergy.

Not surprisingly, the vast majority of victim-survivors have left the Church and have no desire for reconciliation. Others want and need reconciliation. There have been apologies from popes and bishops and some attempts at reconciliation in parishes and dioceses, with healing services and selecting victim-survivors for the Washing of the Feet on Holy Thursday. Notably, in Boston, under Cardinal O'Malley, who has a vast experience of dealing with abuse issues from his work in three different dioceses, there is an Advent Mass every year for victim-survivors and their families. Diocesan and parish outreach programs in some places have offered support. While much good work has been done, the entire Church community has not assumed sufficient responsibility for the harm done. Parishes and families not directly affected by the abuse distance themselves from the problem. There is a challenge for all of us that

> Those harmed by abuse must not be viewed as damaged goods that must be dealt with so that the Church can be done with this mess and begin to move on. Formal apologies, compensation and penalties meet the demands of civil justice, but Jesus requires more. He instructs the shepherd to leave the flock (the ninety-nine) in order to seek out the little one who has been harmed, driven away and abandoned.[11]

2 The Dynamics of Sexual Abuse by Clergy

The sexual abuse of children and youth has occurred throughout history. Until the 1980s, child physical and sexual abuse were unrecognized as a major problem.[12] They were not part of the training of family doctors, paediatricians, social workers, mental health professionals or clergy. Despite enormous advances in understanding the dynamics and consequences of the sexual abuse of children and youth, it remains a major problem in modern society. While the Catholic Church has become the poster child for this problem, sexual abuse of children and youth is most likely to occur in homes by fathers, grandfathers, brothers, cousins and babysitters. It also happens in schools, sports teams and youth activities, where it is perpetrated by teachers, Boy Scout leaders and coaches. In 2011, the abuse scandal at Penn State University in Pennsylvania resulted in the ouster of a long-revered head coach and the University President for lack of oversight. The world of hockey has coped with sexual abuse revelations as well, such as those by the NHL's Sheldon Kennedy, who played for the Calgary Flames and the Boston Bruins. Despite the fact that, for many, the sexual abuse of children and youth remains the only socially unacceptable sexual sin, its prevalence is shocking.

A 2004 report by the John Jay College of Criminal Justice in conjunction with the United States Conference of Catholic Bishops[13] identified 4 percent of active priests as abusers. An extremely small number of religious women offenders have been identified but not studied because of the numbers. This incidence in the Church is no greater than that in society in general, demonstrating that priests are human and subject to the same sins, pathology and vulnerabilities as others. Sexual abuse of children and youth *is* a major social problem in which the Church shares. But that is not the point for a Church that teaches a very high standard of sexual morality in general and a deep commitment to justice, care and concern for the vulnerable.

The incidence of clergy abuse increased from the mid-1960s to late 1970s, and then began an ongoing decline in the 1980s. This decline in society in general and in clergy cases is the result of many factors, including a substantial increase in knowledge about victimization and the harm of sexual abuse as well as increased social vigilance.[14]

The dynamics of clergy abuse

Many ask how stories such as John's could possibly have occurred within the Church. The dynamics of clergy abuse are consistent with David Finkelhors' classic model of sexual abuse of children and youth in general. In order for abuse to occur, there must be motivation to abuse; an overcoming of internal inhibitions; an overcoming of external factors; and, finally, an overcoming of the child or youth's resistance.[15]

The motivation to abuse is often an emotional congruence with the victim. There is a wealth of information about emotional and sexual immaturity of many priests, especially those ordained before the initiation of psychological screening for seminary admission and the introduction of programs of "human formation."[16] Another motivator is a blockage of non-sexual intimate relations with adults. Again, the literature demonstrates unsurprising problems with intimacy for priests who are bound by celibacy and highly scrutinized friendships. "Priests who lacked close social bonds, and those whose family spoke negatively or not at all about sex, were more likely to abuse minors than those who had a history of close social bonds and positive discussions about sexual behaviour."[17]

Even with motivation, there must be an overcoming of strong internal inhibitions to the sexual abuse of children and youth. This requires the creation of excuses and justifications for the abuse: "I'm not doing anything wrong"; "He likes it"; "I am not violating my promise of celibacy because this is not sex with a woman."

There must be the creation of opportunities for abuse to occur. While things have changed considerably, during the peak times of these offences, priests had an almost unlimited access to children and youth, especially boys.

Finally, there must be an overcoming of the child's resistance through grooming techniques. Individuals were made to feel special by the attention from the special person of the priest. This individual grooming was facilitated by the general reverence for and trust in the person of the priest:

> Catholic victims, conditioned by their religious indoctrination, looked on the priest-abuser with a mixture of awe and fear. The cleric's attitude of su-

periority and power elicited emotional security and trust in his victim ... The awe, fear, and wonder experienced by the victim are best described as religious duress ... a fear that is induced from the respect, awe, or reverence one has for an authority figure.[18]

The world of Catholicism, before this abuse crisis broke, created a perfect storm of beliefs and practices where the chaos of sexual abuse wreaked its havoc.

The clergy offenders

What do we know of the clergy who were the direct cause of the pain and suffering of these children and youth? We know some things about who they were and were not. The John Jay College of Criminal Justice study confirms other social science literature in debunking some of the myths of clergy abusers: there is no direct correlation between homosexuality and sexual abuse of children and youth, and there is no direct correlation between mandatory celibacy and sexual abuse of children and youth. Two basic profiles of sexually abusive clergy have been identified: compulsive sexual predators and situational sexual offenders.

Compulsive sexual predators are classified as *pedophiles* where the object of sexual attraction is pre-pubertal children or *ephebophiles* where the object of sexual attraction is early adolescent and post-pubertal youth. While the media identifies all priests as pedophiles, fewer than five percent of priests with allegations of abuse are pedophiles; almost all were ephebophiles. Both offences are gravely harmful to victims, but the distinction is important for treatment. About half of all known cases of clergy abuse are compulsive sexual predators. The other half is composed of situational offenders with confused, conflicted sexuality, loneliness and isolation, and alcohol abuse as the trigger for an abusive event. The John Jay II Study has shown that "Many accused priests began abusing years after they were ordained, at times of increased job stress, social isolation, and decreased contact with peers."[19]

The distinction does not minimize the harm done to children and youth, but it will become important as we look at what must be done to prevent this and other abuses in future. Half of the priest offenders were in high-risk situations where they could have been given support, encouragement and assistance. It presents challenges in our response to the offenders themselves. Forgiveness is central to our faith, but the sin of sexual abuse by clergy, regardless of circumstances, appears as unforgivable.

The pain and suffering revealed here is great, first and foremost for individuals but also for the entire Body of Christ. Denial of the harm and its profound consequences has compounded the harm for all concerned and has created dysfunction and debility. This patient needs help and healing urgently.

3. Gospel Themes that Propose an Alternative

Sexual abuse within the Church is a profound contradiction of the teaching and witness of Christ. —Pope John Paul II[20]

As you read of this history, what contradiction of the teaching and witness of Christ comes to mind? Which scriptures speak to you?

Some that have moved me follow:

› The power and significance of the Nativity:

"Do not be afraid; for see – I am bringing you good news of great joy for all the people: to you is born this day in the city of David a Saviour, who is … wrapped in bands of cloth and lying in a manger." (Luke 2:10-12)

› The care and protection of the child Jesus from Mary and Joseph:

"Get up, take the child and his mother, and flee to Egypt, and remain there until I tell you; for Herod is about to search for the child and destroy him." (Matthew 2:13)

› Jesus lost in the Temple and Mary and Joseph's frenzied search for him:

When he was twelve years old, they went up as usual for the festival. When the festival was ended and they started to return, the boy Jesus stayed behind in Jerusalem, but his parents did not know it. Assuming that he was in the group of travellers, they went a day's journey. Then they started to look for him among their relatives and friends. When they did not find him, they returned to Jerusalem to search for him. (Luke 2:42-45)

› The words of Jesus himself:

"If any of you put a stumbling block before one of these little ones who believe in me, it would be better for you if a great millstone were fastened around your neck and you were drowned in the depth of the sea." (Matthew 18:6)

How does the Word speak to you?

_____

_____

_____

_____

SOME QUESTIONS FOR REFLECTION AND ACTION

- How significant do you think the clergy sexual abuse crisis is in the life of the Church?

- How do you react to these stories of abuse and violation of trust?

- Have you had any direct experience with victim-survivors or clergy-offenders?

- How adequate has our response been to the ongoing needs of victim-survivors?

- What is it about us as Catholics – bishops, priests, and people – that allowed these offences against vulnerable children to go on for so long?

- What can you do to respond to the call of the Lord here?

- What could your parish do?

- What could your diocese do?

CHAPTER 2

A HISTORY OF THE PROBLEM

"So have no fear of them: for nothing is covered up that will not be uncovered, and nothing secret that will not become known. What I say to you in the dark, tell in the light: and what you hear whispered, proclaim from the housetops."
(Matthew 10:26-28)

We will not have a Church which is safe for the young until we learn from Christ and become again a humble Church in which we are equal children of the one Father. —Timothy Radcliffe, OP[1]

Despite all of the high technology of modern medicine available to doctors and patients, appropriate investigation and accurate diagnosis still require a careful history of the onset and progression of illness, disease and disability. This history is crucial to understanding the roots of the problem and to directing attention to factors that must be investigated further. Sometimes, in pressing for details of the medical history, an event or experience that has been ignored or long forgotten is recalled that becomes crucial in the diagnosis. Importantly, the history of attempted treatments can contribute crucial information about the right prescription.

In Chapter 1, we saw some of the history of the abuse of individual victims and the immediate response of leadership to disclosure. That history demonstrates how the response to victims' claims of abuse compounded their victimization and contributed to the second and more pervasive crisis of general mismanagement by Church leadership. This second and ongoing crisis is still with us today. It presents us with a public health–like situation where the risk and harm extend beyond individuals to communities, and where there are many victims. Acknowledging this leadership crisis is essential to understanding the complexity of the larger issue before us, and the depth and breadth of purification and spiritual and ecclesial renewal to which we are called.

Many of us feel that we have heard more than we can bear about this scandal. After all, we have been bombarded by headlines and court cases and criminal charges. Sexual abuse by priests has made it into movies, such as the 2008 award-winning *Doubt*, and into TV dramas, documentaries and specials. Even the sexual decadence of the Borgia Pope has made its way into a mini-series. It is not at all unusual now to have crime shows with priests as primary suspects. Traditional assumptions of innocence of clergy have morphed rapidly into subtle assumptions of guilt.

We all come to this issue with preconceptions and biases. A common understanding of key events and actions in this history is essential for our reflection and meaningful discussion.

Objectives

In this chapter we will

1. review some central events in the history of the sexual abuse of children and youth by Roman Catholic clergy and religious, primarily in North America;
2. analyze some persistent patterns that characterize the response of most Church leaders;
3. share some Gospel images and words that propose an alternative; and
4. suggest some initial questions for reflection and discussion.

1 Some History

Some accounts, including the John Jay *Causes and Contexts* report for the US Catholic bishops,[2] present the issue of clergy sexual abuse of children and youth as a recent phenomenon. They situate the problem within post–Vatican II changes and challenges, the sexual revolution of the 1960s and 1970s, and rising secularism.

In fact, the sexual abuse of children and youth by clergy is almost as old as the Church. From the Council of Elvira in 306 on, it is condemned over and over again in the rules and decrees promulgated before the first code of canon law, the *Corpus Juris Canonici* (12C), appeared.[3]

The *Book of Gomorrah* (1051) by St. Peter Damien contains an explicit outcry against clerical sexual contact with young boys. He appealed to Pope Leo IX to take strong action regarding offending clerics. It has been noted that "Although Peter had paid significant attention to the impact of offending clerics on their victims, the pope focused only on the sinfulness of the clerics and their need to repent."[4] Observe this focus on clerics, not victims, as the beginning of a pattern of response. Numerous canonical policies have been developed to deal with the issue, almost all of them cautioning secrecy to avoid giving scandal to the Church. (See Appendix I at the end of this book.)

We can see three phases in the modern history of this crisis: 1960–1982; 1983–2002, and 2002 to today. Out of the vast array of information now available, some pivotal events and actions are summarized here (See also Appendix II at the end of this book.)

Under Wraps: 1960–1982

In Chapter 1, we saw that the vast majority of offences occurred between 1960 and 1982, but this first phase is characterized by public invisibility. The offences were occurring, but they were being handled by internal Church mechanisms. Public disclosures of clergy sexual abuse of minors began in the US and then in Canada. This happened in large part because victims, often revictimized and frustrated by the Church's internal canonical and bureaucratic responses, pursued legal recourse. Early cases were reported by parents, priests and others who came to know of the offences. By the mid-1990s, cases were being reported by adults years after the abuse occurred. By 2002, reports were being presented by lawyers from victim-survivors from 30 to 40 years ago.

Public Revelations: 1983–2002

In 1983, the issue became public in the case of Fr. Gilbert Gauthe in the Louisiana bayou. Jason Berry and others at the *National Catholic Reporter (NCR)* covered the case. Gauthe was found guilty of eleven charges of child abuse and sentenced to prison. The features of his case became the pattern for many that followed: a charismatic figure with easy access to children and youth; allegations of inappropriate behaviour; some confrontation with Church officials; and then movement to another parish. The *NCR* investigative team, sensing this was not an isolated case, pursued the issue and consolidated a report on other cases emerging in the US, Canada and Ireland in articles in a June 1985 issue.[5]

There was no public statement by the United States Conference of Catholic Bishops (USCCB) after the shocking *NCR* disclosures, but it is reported that the executive discussed the issue. This same year, and on their own initiative, Fr. Thomas Doyle, Fr. Mike Peterson and Ray Mouton, experts in canon law and psychology who had experience in treating priest offenders, prepared a report for the US bishops, known as *The Manual*, on the scope of the abuse crisis. The report was never formally presented to the USCCB, nor was it received by the Conference. It was not until 1988 that the first public statement by US bishops,

the *Pedophilia Statement*,⁶ was issued. It was prepared not by a bishop, but by USCCB legal counsel Mark Chopko. It reads not as a pastoral statement but as an attorney's attempt at damage control. It speaks to abuse as a societal issue, framed within canon and civil law, with no mention of the emerging clergy crisis across the country.

In Canada, following devastating experiences of sexual abuse by Irish Christian Brothers at the Mount Cashel Orphanage, the Archdiocese of St. John's, Newfoundland, was further rocked by allegations against six priests and two former priests and the arrest of the very public Fr. James Hickey, who was charged with 32 counts of sexual misconduct and sent to prison. In 1989, in a remarkable and unprecedented act, Archbishop Alphonsus Penney established the Archdiocesan Commission of Enquiry into the Sexual Abuse of Children by Members of the Clergy to provide independent opinion as to *what* had happened and *why*. In 1990, *The Report of the Archdiocesan Commission of Enquiry into the Sexual Abuse of Children by Members of the Clergy* was released; it concluded that

> … no single cause can account for the sexual abuse … rather, it is the Commission's view that a combination of factors coincided to allow the abuse to occur. Some were direct such as the regressed sexuality of the offenders, their access to children, and the powerful status accorded to priests within the patriarchal Church community. Others were indirect and worked in less obvious ways, some to protect the offenders and inhibit public acknowledgement of the offences.⁷

The Commission identified six themes around these factors that needed further exploration in order to understand the *why*: "power, education, sexuality, support of priests, management, and avoidance of scandal." Contemporary scholars of the crisis have concluded that with this "landmark" Newfoundland Report, "… the initial assumption that these occurrences were rare and isolated events could no longer be sustained."⁸

In Chicago, Cardinal Joseph Bernadin, reacting to his error in reassigning an inadequately assessed priest offender who went on to abuse others, appointed a commission that reported in July 1992. This report began to influence some US bishops' responses to allegations.

In 1992, Fr. James Porter of Fall River, Massachusetts, pleaded guilty to 41 counts of sexual assault and went to prison. Under the new bishop, Sean O'Malley, the Fall River diocese agreed to pay out $7 million to victims. Cardinal Law in neighbouring Boston assured the flock that Porter's acts were not the fault of the Church but "an aberrant act" of one man. Cardinal Law also claimed the media reports had been deliberately overblown because of anti-Catholic bias.

Ten years after the Gauthe case, and with hundreds of allegations of clergy abuse across the country, the first public statement on the problem was issued by a USCCB President, Archbishop Daniel Pilarczyk of Cincinnati. The Bishops formed an Ad Hoc Committee on Sexual Abuse. There was some real, though uneven and incomplete, progress in the US. Cases emerging now were largely historical, most of them beyond the statute of limitations. The Canadian Conference of Catholic Bishops (CCCB) produced *From Pain to Hope*,[9] containing the first published national episcopal guidelines on clergy sexual abuse, and *Breach of Trust, Breach of Faith*,[10] a discussion document for parishes and lay groups that was rarely used. (In most dioceses, it was not used at all.) The USCCB developed its "5 Principles" for responding to abuse: greater openness about allegations; prompt response to allegations; removal of offenders from ministry for evaluation and treatment; compliance with civil law; and outreach to victims and their families.[11] Many bishops did strengthen their responses to allegations, including creating new advisory panels with lay representation.

Although Pope John Paul II had been aware of the scandal since 1983, he did not issue a public statement until his June 1993 Letter to the US bishops. It began with an expression of sympathy for the suffering the scandal had caused them! The victims were given passing reference: "… I fully share your sorrow and concern … especially … for the victims so seriously hurt by these misdeeds."[12] The Pope spoke of the abuse in the context of sin, especially in the materialistic culture of the US; media bias; and the need for prayer. Much of his focus was on the negative effects on priests and bishops, not on the devastating harm to the victims or their families and faith communities.

In Dallas in 1997, a jury awarded a staggering $120 million to eleven victims of Fr. Rudy Kos and, in the decision, indicated disgust with the way the Church kept him in ministry after repeated credible allegations of sexual abuse.

As we entered the new millennium, virtually no diocese in North America was unscathed. There was "evidence that Catholic bishops, with very few exceptions, had not only protected the abusers, but in the process had also breached the procedures of both canon and civil law."[13] The situation in Ireland had erupted and cases were emerging in Europe and Australia.

In 2001, the Vatican revised procedural norms dealing with clerical abuse, requiring cases to be reported to the Congregation for the Doctrine of the Faith (CDF), but still did not require reporting to civil authorities. Oversight of clergy sexual abuse cases came under Cardinal Ratzinger, now Pope Benedict XVI, who diligently reviewed the cases on Fridays. He was said to be so disturbed by the information that he called this his Friday penance. He persuaded Pope John Paul II to send a *motu proprio*, *Sacramentorum Sanctitatis Tutela*,[14] which required

bishops to report all cases of sexual abuse of minors by clergy to Rome for its guidance and the coordination of responses.

2002 to the present

The third and ongoing phase of this crisis began in January 2002, with the *Boston Globe*'s front-page story of the cover-up of repeated sexual abuse of minors by Fr. John Geoghan. The *Globe*'s story asked,

> Since the mid-1990s, more than 130 people have come forward with horrific tales about how former priest John J. Geoghan allegedly fondled or raped them through a three-decade spree through a half-dozen greater Boston parishes. Always his victims were grammar school boys. One was just four years old … There is no dispute that Geoghan abused children at Blessed Sacrament in Saugus after his 1962 ordination … Cardinal Bernard F. Law knew about Geoghan's problems in 1984 … [I]n 1998, the church "defrocked" Geoghan … Why did it take a succession of three cardinals and many bishops 34 years to place children out of Geoghan's reach?[15]

After intense investigations, records showed that more than 90 priests of the diocese had been accused of abuse over the previous 40 years. Boston was the only archdiocese in the US where more than half the population was Catholic; the effects of these revelations were devastating.[16] Not surprisingly, in April 2002, American cardinals were summoned to Rome to discuss what Rome saw as the "American problem." There were tsunami-like consequences in North America and globally. There were unprecedented demands for Church records, overturning previous protection of confidentiality and privilege. Civil suits from incidents 20 and 30 years before emerged, forcing dioceses to sell assets, and at least eight dioceses to declare bankruptcy to settle legal claims.

In June 2002, the USCCB produced its *Charter for the Protection of Children and Young People*.[17] The Charter created a National Review Board (NRB) to assess the causes and context of the crisis. The NRB engaged the John Jay College of Criminal Justice of the City University of New York to conduct research on the issue.

After a huge outcry regarding the mismanagement of cases in Boston, Cardinal Law's resignation was accepted by Pope John Paul II in mid-December 2002. He was not chastised or penalized for his mismanagement. Instead he was appointed Arch-Priest of Saint Mary Major in Rome. His replacement, Cardinal Sean O'Malley, came to Boston with experience. He had dealt with the issue in Fall River, Massachusetts, and Palm Beach, Florida, where he replaced two consecutive bishops who had resigned following revelations of abuse.

In 2004, John Jay College of Criminal Justice produced its report *The Nature and Scope of Sexual Abuse of Minors by Catholic Priests and Deacons in the United*

States.[18] It revealed that more than 4,300 priests were alleged to have abused almost 11,000 victims between 1950 and 2002 – and these were only the reported cases. Approximately one third of all reports to 2004 were made in 2002, after a delay of almost 30 years.

In Canada in August 2009, Bishop Raymond Lahey of Antigonish, Nova Scotia, originally a priest from St. John's, Newfoundland, was hailed for a historic out-of-court settlement worth $15 million for victims of clergy sexual abuse in his diocese. In September, returning from a visit outside the country, he was arrested for possession and importation of child pornography. With this news, Canada reeled. He was subsequently imprisoned and dismissed from the clerical state in 2012. He has since been released after pleading guilty and serving his sentence.

Pope Benedict opened the 2009–2010 Year for Priests, a year with escalating issues of clergy sexual abuse worldwide, with this quote from St. Jean Vianney, known as the *Curé d'Ars*: "After God, the priest is everything!"[19] Throughout that year, priests went off together to study the meaning of priesthood as if the clergy abuse crisis did not exist. The Pope ended the Year for Priests on a different note:

> And so it happened that, in this very year of joy for the sacrament of the priesthood, the sins of priests came to light – particularly the abuse of the little ones, in which priesthood, whose task is to manifest God's concern for our good, turns into the very opposite. We too beg forgiveness from God and from the persons involved, while promising to do everything possible to ensure that such abuse will never occur again ....[20]

On Ash Wednesday 2011, Cardinal Justin Rigali of the Archdiocese of Philadelphia announced suspensions of 27 priests pending investigation of sexual abuse charges. In 2005, a Grand Jury had criticized the archdiocese for its handling of abusive priests, and in 2011, a second Grand Jury concluded that "Cardinal Rigali and his auxiliary bishops also have failed miserably at being open and transparent." His resignation was accepted as Cardinal Law's was, with no admonition or penalty.

In May 2011, in an effort to promote a uniform global standard in response to the abuse crisis, the Congregation for the Doctrine of the Faith issued a Circular Letter with "guidelines" to help deal with cases of clergy sexual abuse. These principles had been articulated in 1992, almost 20 years before, in the CCCB's resource *From Pain to Hope* and in the USCCB's "5 Principles." Part Two of the John Jay College of Criminal Justice study for the USCCB, *Causes and Context*,[21] was published.

In October 2011, Bishop Robert Finn of the Diocese of Kansas City–St. Joseph was indicted by a county grand jury for failure to report suspected child abuse.

This was the first indictment of a sitting US bishop for management of an abuse issue.

In June 2012, Monsignor William J. Lynn of the Archdiocese of Philadelphia was found guilty of child endangerment. He is the first senior Church official in the United States convicted for covering up sex abuse by clergy.

Ireland, Europe and Globally

Clerical abuse and episcopal cover-up, first made public in the US and Canada, began to sprout in Ireland's Ryan[22] and Murphy[23] reports, England and Wales,[24] and Australia.[25] Stories also began emanating from Belgium, France, Germany and the Netherlands.[26]

Ireland, that most Catholic nation, has been particularly devastated by sexual abuse of children and youth by priests and religious.[27] In 2004, the Irish government fell over allegations of complicity with Church cover-up. In 2011, Ireland's President, Enda Kenny, made an emotional statement regarding Church obstacles to disclosures. The Irish Jesuit Seamus Murphy, in looking at the Irish Church, saw a failure by bishops to apply the law, for which they were responsible, to abusers.[28]

At a February 2012 symposium in Rome on the sexual abuse crisis, entitled "Towards Healing and Renewal" and sponsored by the Jesuit Pontifical Gregorian University in collaboration with a number of Vatican departments, Monsignor Stephen Rosetti, former director of St. Luke's Institute in Silver Spring, Maryland, which treats abuser priests, spoke strongly on the global nature of this problem. He told the assembled bishops and leaders of religious congregations that to deny the global issue was to repeat the pattern of denial shown to individual victims.[29]

2 Leadership Response: Identifying Patterns and Themes

The modern history of this problem is almost 30 years old. As it has unfolded publicly, we have had responses from individual bishops, national conferences of bishops, and the Pope himself. It is evident that claims from some that "the Church has done nothing about this crisis" are unfounded. In fact, in recent decades, the Roman Catholic Church, for many reasons, has done more than any other single organization on policies and protocols in this area. The compelling question is: Is this enough?

This brief history and some of the extensive published work on this issue help us identify some themes and patterns in the response of Church leadership. The history of the issue is characterized by denial, minimization of harm to the institutional Church, protection of the priest offender, and preservation of secrecy in order to avoid scandal. These responses, which transcend continents and social cultures, are consistent, despite rising social expectations of transparency and accountability from individuals and institutions. We have been a Church of secrecy and denial in a world of increasing openness and transparency. In a tragic paradox, the need to "avoid scandal" has resulted in the greatest scandal in the modern Church.

The history demonstrates a puzzling, painful aspect of response from leaders and pastors in the Church, from seemingly callous indifference to the pain and suffering of the victims, to outright hostility to them and any "whistleblowers." John Jay investigators, reporting on their massive study for the US Catholic Conference of Bishops, made a particular point of their concern that bishops interviewed about the crisis, including bishops who had serious and multiple offenders in their dioceses, showed little or no concern for the welfare of the children. Neither did these bishops show emotions such as moral outrage, shame, disappointment, and so on that others in the Church feel so strongly. The National Review Board for the Protection of Children and Young People observed, "The lack of expressions of outrage by bishops – both at the time they first learned of the abhorrent acts of some priests and in dealing with the crisis publicly – is troubling."[30]

This pattern was repeated across the Atlantic:

> … the Dublin Archdiocese's pre-occupation in dealing with cases of child abuse, at least until the mid 1990s, were the maintenance of secrecy, the avoidance of scandal, the protection of the reputation of the Church, and the preservation of its assets. All other considerations, including the welfare of children and justice for victims, were subordinated to these priorities.[31]

Bishops generally responded as bureaucrats, not as shepherds. Before 2002, most bishops had little, if any, direct and meaningful contact with victims.

When allegations were made, diocesan leaders generally protected the priest-abuser. Recognizing the need for due process, the responses were handled within the structures – using investigation, evaluation and administrative leave, not criminal law. Formal canonical responses, such as laicization, were complicated and time-consuming, and so were avoided. Many priest offenders were sent away for rehabilitation when no help was offered to victims or their families. The priests were returned to ministry with their reputations intact, even in the face of overwhelming evidence of abuse.

This protection of the priest-offender was most dramatically demonstrated as recently as 2001, when Cardinal Castrillon Hoyos of Colombia, Prefect of the Congregation for the Clergy, wrote a letter to Bishop Pierre Pican of Bayeux-Lisieux, praising him for protecting a priest pedophile: "I rejoice to have a colleague

in the episcopacy who, in the eyes of history and all other bishops of the world, preferred prison rather than denouncing one of his sons, a priest."[32]

Even a cursory review of the history reveals an inordinately slow learning curve regarding the issue. The issue of clergy abuse became public in 1983. Experts offered information on the emerging issue to the USCCB in 1985. The St. John's, Newfoundland, Archdiocesan Commission of Enquiry into the Sexual Abuse of Children by Members of the Clergy Report, which clearly indicated the systemic and cultural nature of the problem, was published in 1990.[33] The CCCB produced guidelines in 1992[34]; USCCB's "5 Principles"[35] were developed in the same year.

In 2002, Boston erupted. It demonstrated failure to take into account much of this earlier work. In 2011, a Philadelphia Grand Jury faulted Cardinal Bevilaqua and others for failing to address the issue appropriately. In October 2011, the first sitting bishop in the US was indicted for failure to report suspected child abuse. In June 2012, Monsignor William J. Lynn of the Archdiocese of Philadelphia was found guilty of child endangerment. He is the first senior Church official in the United States to be convicted for covering up sex abuse by clergy.

Some of the delay in learning happened because bishops reversed the victim and victimizer roles; disparaged critics; shifted blame to parents; or claimed they were given poor information by psychologists and psychiatrists. In other instances, delay clearly related to the instinctive protection of the authority of individual bishops in their own dioceses, which made mandatory standards difficult to enforce. Even standards developed by national episcopal conferences are voluntary.

The history reveals a focus on policies and protocols as the appropriate response to the crisis. The general literature raises deeper systemic and cultural questions. A few leaders who recognize the deeper spiritual and ecclesial issue underlying this crisis have emerged. Early on, the Canadian bishops showed leadership in Newfoundland and nationally. Joseph Cardinal Bernadin of Chicago and others tried to develop more sensitive and compassionate responses to victims. A few others called for attention to the systemic/cultural nature of the crisis and for deep analysis and spiritual and ecclesial transformation. This group includes Diarmuid Martin of Dublin; Robert Zollitsch of Germany; Kevin Dowling of South Africa, Geoffrey Robinson of Australia,[36] and Mark Coleridge of Canberra and Goulburn, Australia. In 2010, Bishop Coleridge courageously presented a cultural and systemic analysis:

> Here I mention briefly several factors which, in my view, may have combined to make the problem cultural rather than merely personal … poor understanding and communication of the Church's teaching on sexuality

… clerical celibacy … has its perils; seminary training; clericalism … triumphalism; … a culture of forgiveness.[37]

Irish bishops responding to the Murphy Report said:

We are deeply shocked by the scale and depravity of the abuse as described in the Report. We are shamed by the extent to which child sexual abuse was covered up in the Archdiocese of Dublin and *recognize that this indicates a culture that was widespread in the Church.*[38]

Pope Benedict XVI, with his experience of the abuse crisis as a former head of the Congregation for the Doctrine of the Faith, has taken a much stronger position and has become more actively involved in this issue than Pope John Paul II did. Bernard Treacy, OP, former editor of *Doctrine and Life*, commenting on Pope Benedict XVI's letter to people of Ireland, has noted that "there is a sense … of a writer overwhelmed by the enormity of what he has had to confront, both in the horror of abuse and in the dereliction of duty among Church leaders to whom it was reported."[39]

The Pope has witnessed to the importance of listening to victims during his many pastoral visits in the United States, Great Britain, Malta, Germany and Australia. In Pope Benedict's many writings and talks on the issue, he has raised it to a major concern for the Church.[40]

We must accept this humiliation as an exhortation to truth and a call to renewal. Only the truth saves … We must ask ourselves what we can do to repair as much as possible the injustice that has occurred. We must ask ourselves what was wrong in our proclamation, in our whole way of living the Christian life, to allow such a thing to happen.[41]

Pope Benedict has promised to "do everything possible to ensure that such abuse will never occur again."[42] However, his focus to date has been on the sins of individual priests, and on policies and protocols. His diagnosis has included the secularization of society, misinterpretations of Vatican II, and the need for prayer. These are all important, but in order to fulfill his promise to "do everything possible to ensure that such abuse will never occur again," the Pope will have to look much deeper into the Church itself. This insight into the depth of the needed renewal seems to have been captured in remarks to the February 2012 conference: "As His Holiness has often observed, healing for victims must be of paramount concern in the Christian community, and it must go hand in hand with a profound renewal of the Church at every level."[43]

The history reveals that there is long-standing and deep pathology here. Denial of the severity of the situation extends from individual offences to patterns of response.

3. Gospel Themes that Propose an Alternative

Sexual abuse within the Church is a profound contradiction of the teaching and witness of Christ. —Pope John Paul II[44]

As you read of this history what contradiction of the teaching and witness of Christ comes to mind? Which scriptures speak to you?

Some that have moved me follow:

- Jesus' words to his disciples on secrecy:

"So have no fear of them: for nothing is covered up that will not be uncovered, and nothing secret that will not become known. What I say to you in the dark, tell in the light: and what you hear whispered, proclaim from the housetops." (Matthew 10:26-27)

- Jesus' words on the community of faith as a body with many different but necessary parts:

Speaking the truth in love, we must grow up in every way into him who is the head, into Christ, from whom the whole body, joined and knit together by every ligament with which it is equipped, as each part is working properly, promotes the body's growth in building itself up in love. (Ephesians 4:15-16)

How does the Word speak to you?

_____

_____

_____

_____

SOME QUESTIONS FOR REFLECTION AND ACTION

- Do you think this history of response to the abuse crisis has implications for you?

- What do you feel about the secrecy and lack of accountability in this history?

- Has the focus on sin and forgiveness, rather than crime and punishment, distorted our sense of justice?

- Have you had experience of raising issues and concerns about the Church?
  If so, what response did you receive?
  If not, can you see yourself doing so in the future?

- What do you believe is needed to restore the Church's credibility as a witness to justice and compassion rather than just another institution misusing power?

- What can you do to respond to the call of the Lord here?

- What could your parish do?

- What could your diocese do?

CHAPTER 3

MECHANISMS OF DISEASE AND ACCURATE DIAGNOSIS

Jesus said, "Those who are well have no need of a physician, but those who are sick." (Matthew 9:12)

We must accept this humiliation as an exhortation to truth and a call to renewal. Only the truth saves ... We must ask ourselves what we can do to repair as much as possible the injustice that has occurred. We must ask ourselves what was wrong in our proclamation, in our whole way of living the Christian life, to allow such a thing to happen. —Pope Benedict XVI[1]

After a patient has described their pain or distress and the doctor has taken a history and assessment of the patient, the doctor is expected to make a diagnosis and prescribe a cure. There is always the danger that the symptoms experienced by the patient, such as pain or weakness, become the focus of attention and the underlying cause is ignored. Symptomatic relief can be a real benefit for a while. Tragically, we know that when the underlying causes and diagnosis have not been properly identified, symptomatic relief can prove dangerous, even fatal. For example, treating a headache as if it was caused by tension, when the real diagnosis is a brain tumour, will result in more pain and suffering and can have fatal consequences.

In reality, the doctor's task of accurate diagnosis and proper prescription has just begun when the history taking and patient assessment are done. The history and symptoms give important clues to the general health of the patient and to the nature of the present problem – the mechanism of disease at work. Different mechanisms of disease, such as trauma, infection and cancer, require different approaches to investigation.

Trauma, such as a fall, can occur to a perfectly healthy individual or to someone who is debilitated by osteoporosis and aging. The effects of trauma are intensified when the individual is not healthy. Basically, trauma comes from outside the individual; the focus of investigation is on treating the effects of the trauma and assessing risks for re-injury. An infection, too, can affect a previously well person or one who is debilitated. Infections, like trauma, come from outside the individual but, once infected, the whole body is involved. Investigation here can be difficult, because the source of the infection may be difficult to locate. Cancer is a more complicated mechanism of disease as it is generally multi-factorial. There are clear internal risk factors for many cancers, such as genetic family history, as well as triggers to activate cancer, such as environmental pollution. Cancer is experienced as an all-consuming process from within the patient.

While taking the patient history requires careful objectivity, the doctor has to make some judgments about possible mechanisms of disease in order to focus investigations. So, some tentative diagnoses, including the most serious possibilities and the most likely causes, are identified. These judgments guide investigation. Patients can become very impatient during this time, but while some things are fairly simple and easily diagnosed, others require careful investigation before an accurate diagnosis can be made.

So, in trying to contribute to the health and healing of the Church, we need to make some assessment of the nature of the ill health in order to guide our further investigation and reflection.

Objectives

In this chapter we will
1. try to identify the underlying causes and nature of the abuse crisis;
2. assess some diagnoses offered by others and their proposed treatments;
3. share some Gospel images of a prophetic alternative; and
4. propose some initial questions for reflection and discussion.

1 The Nature of the Crisis

How we understand the nature of the crisis depends in large part on what we consider the normal health of the Church to be. Some Catholics claim this is not a crisis of the basic health of the Church. Rather, they claim, the situation has been contrived by the media and fostered by greedy lawyers and victim-survivors who are out to make money. The sexual abuse of children and youth by members of the Roman Catholic clergy has become a case of what is known as "moral panic." This occurs when a situation, person or group of persons becomes identified as a particular social threat. The term "predator priests" is a manifestation of this phenomenon.[2] It creates a false sense of risk and danger from all priests. Many other Catholics acknowledge that there has been abuse, but see it as no more of a problem in the Church than in society in general. For them, the issue has been exaggerated, and Roman Catholic clergy have become scapegoats.

However, virtually all of the many serious theological, psychological and criminological analyses judge this to be a true crisis for the health and holiness of the Church. The gravity of the problem is acknowledged, but the nature of the underlying pathology is contested.

As we saw in Chapter 1, for individual victim-survivors, the fundamental nature of the problem is a sexual assault. However, because the assailant is a man of God, it is also a spiritual assault, and the response of Church leaders to the revelations has further eroded trust in God and in the Church.

Interestingly, many of those who have reflected on the crisis more broadly have used the language of mechanisms of disease to describe this situation. Trauma, infection and cancer are frequently used metaphors in formal analysis and in news headlines. These analogies intuitively capture different understandings of both the causes and consequences of the abuse crisis.

It is not surprising that there have been many different diagnoses of the fundamental nature of the clergy sexual abuse crisis. A critical analysis of these diagnoses is needed in this especially divisive time in our Church. Internal division and dissension between liberal and conservative Catholics, Latin Mass (even Tridentine Rite) Catholics, Vatican II Catholics, charismatic Catholics, and so on, is having profound effects on the life and health of the Church. There is a great temptation to use this crisis to move particular liberal or conservative agendas for the Church. Conservatives want to treat their pain over issues of orthodoxy, fidelity and obedience. Liberals want a remedy for their pain over mandatory celibacy, limitations on the role of women and general non-involvement of the laity in the life of the Church. There is a real danger of paying attention to symptoms rather than deeper diagnosis. In a real sense, the public exposé of this crisis has occurred at a time in Church history when malaise and tension affect the general health of the Church. The Church is experiencing this crisis not from a position of robust health but in a debilitated state.

Here we will review some of the analyses of the nature of this crisis and the prescriptions that follow those analyses.

For many Catholics, this is a crisis of *authority*. Bishops and other Church leaders simply did not do their jobs – to teach, govern and sanctify. Shockingly, they did not even enforce the canon law of the Church in most cases.[3] This assessment makes apparent the lack of formal mechanisms of accountability to the faithful in the Church. All canonical accountability is vertical: from priests to bishops and from bishops to the Pope.

Another position is articulated by conservative columnist George Weigel. He understands the issue as multi-faceted, but identifies it as a crisis of *infidelity*. It is about the sexual sins of individuals and the neglect of bishops, but is also about seminary professors; priests who doubt; theologians who encourage a "culture of dissent"; undue attention to the social sciences; and the acceptance of homosexuality.[4] Weigel presumes a time, pre–Vatican II, of great piety, obedience and integrity, which eroded in the 1960s with widespread dissent from *Humanae Vitae*, Pope Paul VI's 1968 encyclical on the issue of birth control. This dissent, Weigel believes, led to a crisis of fidelity and moral authority and ultimately to the sexual abuse of children and youth, so his remedy demands courage, clarity, vigilance, obedience, zeal and unwavering loyalty.

For a substantial number of Catholics, this is a crisis of *lust and sexuality*, with at least three different interpretations. For some of them, the Church has not been aggressive enough on enforcing sexual teachings or on keeping all sexual activity within marriage. The sexual liberation of the 1960s and 1970s is to blame, they feel, so the prescription is clearly to hold all to chastity, teach with greater clarity on every aspect of human sexuality, and enforce the teaching. Others believe a repressive approach to sexuality and to women contributed to secretive and distorted sexual activity. Their prescription is a renewal regarding sexuality that includes all – clergy, lay, celibate, married, single – in the dialogue. Yet another interpretation sees *mandatory celibacy*, with its aura of the supernatural, suggesting a holier state of priests than of laity, and loneliness and sexual immaturity in the lives of priests, as problematic.[5]

Feminist analysis sees *patriarchy* – understood as a social system in which the male role as primary authority is a central feature – as causative of the crisis. In a patriarchal system such as the Roman Catholic Church, females are subordinated to males and the relational wisdom of women is lost from discernment and decision making.[6] Some propose that feminist theology has crucial insights that are necessary for the real, active participation of all in the life and work of the Church.[7]

Social science analyses have positioned this as a crisis of *trust* in the institution. This is not just a loss of trust in individuals, but is understood as a "structural betrayal of trust."[8] One social scientist, focusing on the loss of faith, hope and trust, suggests that

> These losses are occasioned by (a) misunderstanding of the nature and use of authority, power and privilege particularly on the part of the bishops and those who appointed them, (b) unwillingness to engage intellectually

with the modern world and its scholarly disciplines, particularly the natural and social sciences, and (c) lack of emotional closeness, basic empathy or a generous and compassionate spirit in relating to the ordinary experiences of human beings.[9]

Real authority – moral authority in contrast to institutional power – is based on recognition of authenticity and integrity in the person, on respect and the ability to elicit trust, and not on rules and regulations. Church leadership will need to demonstrate the transparency, humility, integrity and truthfulness expected of other professionals and of their calling, if they are to regain trust. Establishing trust is the focus of the National Federation of Catholic Youth Ministry,[10] as persons who are under 30 years of age have been exposed to this crisis their whole lives. For them, the issue is not restoring trust in the Church and its leadership. It is in building that trust.

Finally, following the general literature on sexual abuse of children and youth, this crisis is understood as *abuse of power*. In the Church context, the particular form of abuse of power arises from the distortion of clericalism, which is a belief that clerics are superior to the laity.[11]

Each of these assessments has merit. But they demonstrate two fundamentally different approaches to understanding the nature of the abuse crisis.

The first approach believes that the Church is in basically sound health. It has been affected by forces from without, which have facilitated the crisis and magnified its effects. The remedy is the restoration of institutional integrity through obedience, orthodoxy and conformity with policies and protocols.

The second approach judges that the debilitated Church of the 21st century is suffering from some long-standing and deep-rooted ill health with some fundamental cultural and systemic concerns. This debilitated state manifested itself in the incredibly slow and lethargic response to this crisis and in the focus, when it did respond, on symptoms rather than underlying causes. This approach recognizes that there is no easy remedy and that more investigation is needed in order to understand the real state of the health of the Church. At the very least, the remedy will require recommitment to continuing the mission of Jesus Christ, the restoration of moral integrity, and the building of relationships of justice and compassion.

2 Assessing Some Proposed Remedies

Many have criticized the Church for "doing nothing" about the abuse crisis. This conclusion is simply not true. We saw in Chapter 2 that there has been much work done in many jurisdictions. The remedies employed to date by Church leadership include

- apologies, including the Pope's;
- improved communication and lay involvement in assessing allegations;
- preventive measures, including improved screening and education of seminarians, protocols for response to allegations, and policies to create safe ministry environments;
- financial compensation for victim-survivors.

Each of these remedies demonstrates an implicit judgment of the nature of the crisis.

We live in an era of public apology. There have been public apologies to Japanese Canadians for internment during the Second World War; to First Nations peoples for the damage done by residential schools; and to the American public for the Gulf of Mexico oil spill. We have heard apologies about sexual abuse from the Pope and from many bishops in dioceses touched by scandal. In one of his apologies, as we saw earlier, Benedict XVI said, "We too beg forgiveness from God and from the persons involved, while promising to do everything possible to ensure that such abuse will never occur again …."[12]

What is the meaning of an apology for something you personally did not do? In the case of the Church, apology by leadership surely implies an acknowledgement of communal and institutional responsibility and guilt. This aspect is not easily found in statements by Church leaders. Meaningful apology requires repentance, restitution and a firm purpose of amendment.

Over the past 30 years, communication on this issue has improved considerably. Much of it has been in response to increased social scrutiny and imposed legal requirements. However, we still see difficulties with openness and transparency. A notable example was the highly publicized problems with the Archdiocese of Philadelphia's sexual abuse review board.[13] There the issue of limited formal authority of lay boards was clearly demonstrated when a Grand Jury investigated serious allegations of clerical sexual abuse that had never been presented to the diocesan board or had been presented with limited information. Openness and transparency don't come easily to the Church.

Preventive measures have included improvements to the screening of candidates for ordination; the inclusion of programs of human formation, with explicit components on human sexuality in the education of seminarians; protocols for managing allegations; and policies for developing safe ministry environments.

While psychological testing and other screening of potential ordinands are now the norm, they were a long time coming.[14] Many Church leaders are highly dependent on psychological screening to detect tendencies to the sexual abuse of children and youth even as there is research information regarding the limited efficacy of screening for sexual predators.[15] Clearly, education regarding sexuality is crucial, but it was not until Pope John Paul II's Letter *Pastores Dabo Vobis* in 1992[16] that seminary education added human development education. These programs were substantially increased after the issuance of the USCCB's Program of Priestly Formation in 2006.[17]

There are, however, ongoing concerns regarding the teaching philosophy and methods used in some of these programs, as well as the role of women in seminary formation. Coursework is but one element in the formation of priests for a healthy sexuality and mature interpersonal relationships with men and women. Noted expert on North American seminary formation Sister Katarina Schuth has noted,

> Theological faculties, who are themselves now more diverse than ever, need to model for students ways of overcoming problems of relationship. Required is humble acceptance of the fact that several approaches to theological questions and pastoral issues are possible and even desirable. Achieving a balance that respects both experience and new insights, as well as having a keen understanding of the ministerial situations for which students are preparing, takes time and commitment.[18]

Protocols for the management of allegations have been in development since 1992, when the CCCB produced *From Pain to Hope*[19] and the USCCB developed its "5 Principles"[20] and published its Charter for the Protection of Children and Young People.[21] Individual dioceses have refined these protocols and used them in various ways. There are still major difficulties with these protocols, which were developed by national conferences of bishops, being "voluntary" in individual dioceses. While there are legitimate concerns regarding protection of priests from unfounded allegations, the resistance to enforcing protocols is deeply problematic and has often resulted in damage to new victims.

In parallel with protocols for management of allegations, policies for developing safe ministry environments have also been developed in most North American dioceses. There are claims that the Catholic Church now has the safest environment for children and youth because of these protocols.

In keeping with this focus on policies and protocols, a symposium for all bishops and religious superiors entitled "Towards Healing and Renewal" was held in February 2012 at the Pontifical Gregorian University in Rome. The US-based VIRTUS program[22] demonstrated some best practices in these areas. Follow-up will include creation of a new Center for Child Protection to develop an e-learning course in abuse prevention and detection in English, German, Italian and Spanish. In addition, the Vatican issued new requirements for diocesan protocols based on the broad principles of victim support, safe environments, and cooperation with police and other civil authorities. Speakers at the symposium called for greater episcopal accountability and warned that the full global nature of this crisis has not yet been made manifest. This symposium represents an important step for the Church in the prevention and management of individual cases of abuse. However, neither Cardinal William Levada, Prefect of the Congregation for the Doctrine of the Faith, who gave the opening address,[23] nor Cardinal Marc Ouellet, Prefect of the Congregation of Bishops, who gave the homily for the penitential Vigil during the symposium,[24] directly addressed the systemic and cultural reasons underlying the mismanagement of the crisis.

Financial compensation and payment for counselling for victim-survivors, generally compelled by lawsuit or by mediation, has been provided as a kind of restitution. There are concerns about the adequacy of finances alone to meet the needs of victim-survivors, especially their spiritual needs. At the same time, the expenditure of diocesan monies in settlements and the sale of diocesan properties have been difficult and contentious for laity. This situation creates an environment that is not conducive to deal with the issues of forgiveness and reconciliation for individuals, parishes or diocesan communities. Victim-survivors are often unjustly perceived as part of an ongoing problem.

Church leadership and the nature of the crisis

These policies and protocols are important remedies for aspects of the abuse crisis, particularly those relating to the abuse of individuals. The focus of these remedies has been almost exclusively on the sins of individual men – priests and bishops – who offended and on priests, bishops and others who minimized the harms to victim-survivors and mismanaged the issue.

We don't always make necessary distinctions between the abuse of individual children and young people by individual offenders, the culture of silence and cover-up about the abuse, and the perceived lack of accountability at the leadership level in how the crisis has been handled. When the distinctions are not made, it is difficult to address adequately all the issues at stake. We have made some progress on the first issue, but the hierarchy, with notable exceptions, is still resistant to take on the issues of the culture of denial, secrecy and avoidance of scandal; Church leadership; and systemic causes for the crisis. Leadership response fits with the assessment that the Church is basically in sound health: that it has been affected by forces from without, which have facilitated the crisis and magnified its effects. The remedy, from this point of view, is the restoration of institutional integrity through obedience, orthodoxy and conformity with policies and protocols.

This approach is clearly seen in the responses of Cardinal Sean O'Malley when interviewed on the tenth anniversary of the *Boston Globe* revelations of abuse cover-up in Boston. John Allen of the *National Catholic Reporter*, in a January 6, 2012, interview, asked O'Malley, given all his past dealings with the abuse issue in Fall River (Massachusetts), Palm Beach (Florida) and Boston:

> NCR: Have these experiences ever tempted you to think there's something wrong with the church that we just can't fix?
>
> O'Malley: *Well, the church is very human, and in every generation there are different manifestations of that. I've been close to the church my whole life. I've seen that humanity. Even as a child, I remember we had a priest in the parish who was an alcoholic and had terrible problems with drinking. The pastor would lock the door of the rectory at 8 p.m., and when he would come home drunk, my father and other men in the parish would take care of him. I think it helped me to understand that priests are human.*
>
> NCR: You never thought, even for a moment, that there's a fatal flaw in the church revealed by this crisis?
>
> O'Malley: *I don't think the Lord is going to abandon his church. We're certainly burdened by our sinfulness, our weakness, and our humanity, but the church is still the sacrament of Christ.*[25]

Clearly, the Cardinal believes this crisis is about individual sins and failings.

This review highlights that there are indeed competing understandings of the nature of this crisis. Church leadership, in general, has focused on the authority/fidelity/obedience diagnosis. Yet there are glimpses of a deeper diagnosis, such as when Pope Benedict suggests, "We must ask ourselves what was wrong in our proclamation, in our whole way of living the Christian life, to allow such a thing to happen."[26]

Bishop Coleridge of Australia has identified

> factors which, in [his] view, may have combined to make the problem cultural rather than merely personal: … poor understanding and communication of the Church's teaching on sexuality; … clerical celibacy … has its perils; seminary training; clericalism; … triumphalism; … [a] culture of forgiveness.[27]

The Irish bishops specifically identify the culture of the Church as a factor:

> We are deeply shocked by the scale and depravity of the abuse as described in the Report. We are shamed by the extent to which child sexual abuse was covered up in the Archdiocese of Dublin and *recognize that this indicates a culture that was widespread in the Church.*[28]

Thankfully, some bishops, including my own, Archbishop Anthony Mancini of Halifax-Yarmouth, have a deep sense that we need to ask ourselves and the Lord some serious questions. As we saw earlier, Mancini wrote to the Catholics of his province, Nova Scotia,

> Why Lord? What does all this mean? What are you asking of me and my priests? What do you want to see happen among your people? Is this a time of purification or is it nothing more than devastation? Are people going to stop believing, will faithful people stop being people of faith? Lord, what are you asking of us and how can we make it happen?[29]

In contrast to the general leadership response, the now vast and diverse literature strongly supports the notion of deeper diagnosis and the need for investigation of systemic and cultural factors that allowed this crisis to unfold as it has and for as long as it has. One such theological analysis emanating from the tragedy in Ireland concludes that the issues at the heart of this crisis include

> (1) the theology of the body and sexuality that has framed Catholic ethics; (2) the related endemic patriarchy that facilitated such a cavalier neglect of children; and (3) the many ecclesiological issues, including the concept of authority, the nature of ministry, and the role of the laity.[30]

An accurate diagnosis of this crisis, essential for any effective treatment, requires that we look in depth at relationships, at the use and abuse of power in the Church, and at morality and sexuality in Catholic life and thought for their effects on the shape and scope of this crisis. We need to reflect together on these issues further, because, in Pope Benedict XVI's words, "Only by examining carefully the many elements that gave rise to the present crisis can a clear-sighted diagnosis of its causes be undertaken and effective remedies … be found."[31]

This is clearly a situation with many elements requiring some in-depth analysis. Single, simple answers won't lead us to healing.

3. Gospel Themes that Propose an Alternative

Sexual abuse within the Church is a profound contradiction of the teaching and witness of Christ.—Pope John Paul II[32]

As you read of this history, what contradiction of the teaching and witness of Christ comes to mind? Which scriptures speak to you?

Some that have moved me follow:

- Jesus taught with authority because of his personal integrity, not his position:

Jesus entered the synagogue and taught. They were astounded at his teaching, for he taught them as one having authority, and not as the scribes. (Mark 1:21-22)

- Jesus' righteous indignation at arrogant claims in the face of moral blindness:

- *Jesus said to [some Pharisees], "If you were blind, you would not have sin. But now that you say, 'We see,' your sin remains."* (John 9:40-41)

On true leadership:

Jesus said to the crowds and to his disciples, "… do whatever [the scribes and the Pharisees] teach you and follow it, but do not do as they do, for they do not practise what they preach. They tie up heavy burdens, hard to bear, and lay them on the shoulders of others; but they themselves are unwilling to lift a finger to move them." (Matthew 23:1-3)

How does the Word speak to you?

_____

_____

_____

_____

4. SOME QUESTIONS FOR REFLECTION AND ACTION

- What do you think have been the most important steps the Church has taken?

- What feelings arise when you think of responses to date:

  – apologies

  – policies for handling allegations

  – protocols for safe ministry environments

  – improved screening of seminary candidates

  – human formation for seminarians

  – financial compensation to victims

- From your experience, what more is needed for us to recover from this crisis and move to renewal?

- What can you do to respond to the call of the Lord here?

- What could your parish do?

- What could your diocese do?

CHAPTER 4

THE ANATOMY OF THE CRISIS: RELATIONSHIPS, POWER AND CLERICALISM

"Let the same mind be in you that was in Christ Jesus, who ... emptied himself, taking the form of a slave..." (Philippians 2:5-6)

"... learn from me; for I am gentle and humble in heart" (Matthew 11:29)

For the distinctions which the Lord made between sacred ministers and the rest of the People of God entails a unifying purpose, since pastors and the other faithful are bound to each other by a mutual need. —Pope Paul VI[1]

After obtaining a careful review of the patients' symptoms and history, the doctor will make some tentative judgments of the nature and mechanisms of disease in order to plan further investigations. These tentative judgments will guide the investigation. If the mechanism is unclear, then the approach will be planned to look at basic causes first and move to more complex investigations after an initial survey. The most basic of these assessments looks at the general state of the patient's anatomy and physiology for clues as to what is wrong. Anatomy is the basic structure of the human body. It includes the skeleton, which provides the physical structure, and all the organs and body parts that make up the complicated network that is the human body.

In the clergy sexual abuse crisis, that anatomy is the fundamental culture and structure of the Church itself. Understanding that culture, structure and the nature of relationships within it appears essential to identifying underlying causes and future prevention of this and similar crises.

Objectives

In this chapter we will

1. describe some general features of the culture and structure of the Roman Catholic Church;
2. identify the abuse of power in the Church known as clericalism and its role in the abuse crisis;
3. share some Gospel images of a prophetic alternative; and
4. propose some initial questions for reflection and discussion.

1. The Culture and Structure of the Church

When we think of culture, we generally think of national cultures: for example, Italian culture or Celtic culture. We might also think of the culture of sports or entertainment. Culture is a complex reality. There is a robust literature on the notion of culture and on the rich and complex relationships between culture and faith. It is not possible to deal with this topic fully here, but some reflection is necessary. One description of culture is an essentially meaningful arrangement of society (*relationships*), ideology (*ways of thinking and valuing*) and technology (*means regarding material things*).² Relationships, values and means reinforce each other. In particular, the arrangement of these three elements shapes the use of power and authority.

The Jesuit George Wilson has provided us with invaluable insights about cultures. These insights help make sometimes abstract-sounding concepts real and understandable. Fr. Wilson states that cultures are embodied ways of thinking and behaving that shape a people; they are not just major activities and events but the ordinary language, behaviour and rituals of daily life; cultures are both empowering and limiting as they tell us what to value, how to behave, and to whom we should listen. He reminds us that cultures are highly resistant to change because cultures generate meaning-security, roots and identity.³

Pope Benedict XVI has brought special attention to the notion of culture in his call to those of us in Western nations to a New Evangelization, which requires a careful examination of how we have all been co-opted by today's culture of individualism, greed, secularism, abuse of power and lack of commitment. The abuse crisis calls for reflection on the culture *of* and *in* the Church, especially for relationships of power. National and ethnic cultures shape our relationships, values and choices, but the culture of the Church transcends even those influences. We need to understand this culture and its use of power and authority if we are to get to an accurate diagnosis of, and treatment for, the abuse crisis.

Here we cannot go into this culture in depth, but we need to think of some of its key relationships, values and means of achieving goals as we reflect on power and authority. While relationships are primarily defined by our baptism and our common calling as brothers and sisters in Christ, our experience is of relationships sharply categorized as ordained or lay and expressed in hierarchical terms. The culture of the Church is highly clericalized.

While the terms "cleric," "clergy" and "clerical" have become associated with religious institutions, the terms actually refer to the sociological reality that all large organizations organize themselves into classes with special power and authority or knowledge and skills. Clerks/clergy are differentiated from ordinary members by special powers, knowledge and status. Medicine, law and politics, to name a few modern institutions, all have obvious members of a "clergy." Large organizations and institutions need clerks/clergy in order to function. What is at issue in the health of an organization is the role and status accorded to the clergy and the nature of the relationship between clergy and laity.

So we need to distinguish at least three interrelated realities here: the Church has and needs a clergy; there is a clerical culture in the Church; and there is a clericalization of the whole Church, with the codification of the distinction between clergy and laity over time.

In the narrow sense, "clerical culture is precisely the constellation of relationships and the universe of ideas and material reality in which diocesan priests and bishops exercise their ministry and spend their lives."[4]

This culture has changed substantially since the initial revelations of the abuse crisis. Many priests now live alone; there is little mentoring by senior clergy of the newly ordained; many priests serve multiple parishes; and there is a sharp divide between priests ordained in the Vatican II theology and those ordained since the installation of Pope John Paul II.[5]

More broadly, the whole Church is clericalized, and the distinction between clergy and laity has become a central feature. While clergy represent only .0004 percent of the worldwide Catholic population, they hold all the power and authority. That clearly situates the culture of the Church as both hierarchical and clerical. Since all clergy are male, the culture is male-dominated. The maintenance of this culture requires both a leadership and a laity who participate in the culture.

Because abuse of power and special status are central to the clergy abuse crisis, we need to understand how clergy achieved this power and status. The history of the Church demonstrates a particular development of those cultural components of *relationships, thinking and valuing, and means* regarding the status, role and function of the clergy and its distinction from the laity. Here, we will highlight a few important points from that history.

HOW DID THE CLERGY–LAITY DISTINCTION BECOME A CHARACTERISTIC OF CATHOLICISM?

Distinctions between clergy and laity were unheard of in the early Church. There, only Jesus is referred to as *priest*. The cultic sacrifices of priests in other religions were understood to have been completed in the ultimate sacrifice of the High Priest, Jesus. Early Christians met in familiar and intimate spaces of upstairs rooms and houses for reflection on ministry and for sharing of the Eucharistic meal. The primary elder or presbyter presided over the meal.

> Ministry in the ancient church is all about action, not cultic worship. Outward moving evangelization, preaching, teaching, and assembly leadership are the core ministries that constitute the Christian way of life. These actions, fundamentally the way a Christian lives his or her life, comprise the sacrifice, the liturgy, and the common priestly office of the whole people.[6]

> The early Christian community is a *diakonia*, or service community, gifted through baptism with charisms for the sake of the whole Church.

> Now there are varieties of gifts, but the same Spirit; and there are varieties of services, but the same Lord; and there are varieties of activities, but it is the same God who activates all of them in everyone. To each is given the manifestation of the Spirit for the common good. (1 Corinthians 12:4-7)

> The gifts of all were valued and clearly understood to be needed by the Church.

> By the end of the first century, individuals in the Christian community come to form the *clerus*, the Lord's portion or share, designating a group for spiritual and leadership functions in the growing community. The first use of laity, as distinct from clergy, appears in the First Letter from Clement at the end of the first century, and then not again until Clement of Alexandria uses it in the *Didascalia Apostolorum*. By the fourth and fifth centuries, the distinction becomes fixed. Constantine's Edict of Milan in 313 makes Christianity the state religion and there is a phenomenal increase in Church membership. The Eucharist moves from homes and intimate spaces into large imperial buildings, which become the basilica churches to accommodate the crowds. As with all large organizations, we see the development of a clergy and a hierarchy. Bishops become officials of the Roman Empire. *Ordinatio*, a Roman term for appointing to Roman civil office, is now used for the priests. As centuries pass, "We have here the beginning of a great

reversal: symbols and legal positions dispensed grace rather than grace begetting life through charisms realized in office and service."⁷

By the time of the Council of Nicea in 325, bishops have increasing power and presbyters shift from being advisors to the Bishop to helpers in the celebration of Eucharist. Presiders over the Eucharist are increasingly understood in priestly/sacrificial terms. By the fifth century, priests are understood almost exclusively in their cultic role and the Eucharist is celebrated in large basilica that separate priests in the sanctuary from people in the pews. The Eucharist becomes more inward and focused on the presider as sacredness and mystery are emphasized. It is removed from the people as the priest is regarded as the only one holy enough to approach the "sacred mysteries." Proximity to the Eucharist comes to mean that ordination to priesthood conveys a permanent indelible character that changes the man's essence. The Council of Florence in 1439 first mentions an "ontological" change in the priest as a result of ordination. This exalted, essentially different character of the priest is captured in the 1566 *Catechism of the Council of Trent*:

> In the first place, then the faithful should be shown how great is the dignity and excellence of this sacrament considered in its highest degree, the priesthood. Bishops and priests being, as they are, God's interpreters and ambassadors, empowered in his name to teach mankind the divine law and rules of conduct and holding, as they do, His place on earth, it is evident that no nobler function than theirs can be imagined. Justly therefore are they called not only Angels but even gods, because of the fact that they exercise in our midst the power and prerogatives of the immortal God.⁸

Bishops and priests as angels and even gods! This appears to be a remarkable contrast to the witness of Jesus himself.

> … though he was in the form of God,
> [he] did not regard equality with God
> as something to be exploited,
> but emptied himself, taking the form of a slave,
> being born in human likeness.
> And being found in human form,
> he humbled himself,
> and became obedient to the point of death—
> even death on a cross. (Philippians 2:6-8)

The requirement for mandatory celibacy in the Western Church emphasizes this angelic designation and understanding of priest as one who is

fundamentally different in nature to other human beings. From the Council of Elvira in 305, clergy were required to abstain from sex with their wives before assisting at the altar. Cultic purity had become crucial. Not surprisingly, then, "Celibacy, in this worldview, is the natural complement to the perfection of the ordained who are closest to the Eucharist and different in kind over the laity."[9]

Lateran Council IV in 1215 mandates celibacy across the Western Church. There were also practical reasons for celibacy, related to the cleric's property and no progeny to inherit or heirs to contest hierarchical authority and power, but cultic purity figured strongly in the decision.

So, the first thousand years of the Church witnessed an inexorable separation of clergy and laity; the second thousand years have confirmed this separation.[10] We also saw the separation of celebration of the Eucharist and ministry and the rejection of the theology of the gifts of all. The laity, the non-ordained, is reduced to the role of observers of the life of the Church.[11]

The fact that Pope Benedict opened the 2009–2010 Year for Priests, a year that saw escalating issues of clergy sexual abuse worldwide, with the quote "After God, the priest is everything!"[12] demonstrates that the clericalization of the Church is alive and well. Throughout that year, priests went off together to study the meaning of priesthood, as if it could be understood without the participation of the laity. The sense of mutual interdependence is replaced by an exalted priestly status. Small wonder that priests and bishops considered themselves above the law in the case of clergy sexual abuse, and that laity defer to them as holier and of special status.

This is the culture we have inherited. The history of the distinction between ordained and lay gives clear examples of, among other things, why mutuality between ordained and lay and between men and women is a rare characteristic of relationships in the Church. The Second Vatican Council attempted a retrieval of the Gospel and the early Church vision,[13] but it has encountered much opposition.

Cultures and their relationships and values are crucial for human identity. They contain within them positive and nourishing elements. But they contain a dark side as well. The Jesuit Michael Paul Gallagher puts it this way:

A culture involves observable practices or socially legitimated ways of acting but it also entails a more concealed set of subjective attitudes often assimilated unconsciously over a long time. Together these habits of acting and interpreting can either imprison people within prejudices or they can become avenues towards authentic living, towards self-transcending choices that challenge the negative bias of any culture.[14]

Identifying the negative bias of a culture becomes challenging, if not impossible, for those inside it. Importantly, being inside a culture can make it very difficult to acknowledge that we ourselves are affected by the negative bias. Just think of the upset and defensiveness we show when others call us "racist" or "sexist." We can be blind to the "isms" or distortions in our own culture. But we are all responsible for our culture.

2 Clericalism and Its Role in the Abuse Crisis

This clerical culture of the Church supports a structure where the distortion of clericalism thrives. Clericalism is about a distorted and inappropriate understanding of the role and function of the clergy. It has facilitated and sustained the clergy abuse crisis. Its toxic and corrosive effects on a healthy structure and on healthy relationships need to be identified clearly for its role in this crisis.

"Clericalism is grounded in the erroneous belief that clerics form a special elite and, because of their powers as sacramental ministers, they are superior to the laity."[15] The Church is ever at risk of clericalism precisely because of the clerical culture of the Church. Among other things, clericalism conflates the holiness of the state of priesthood with the holiness of the individual priest. In another analysis,

> Clericalism is the conscious or unconscious concern to protect the particular interests of the clergy and to protect the privilege and power that traditionally has been conceded to those in the clerical state ... Among its chief manifestations are an authoritarian style of ministerial leadership, a rigidly hierarchical worldview, and a virtual identification of the holiness and grace of the church with the clerical state and thereby with the cleric himself.[16]

Fr. George Wilson has provided a very thoughtful analysis of the characteristics of clericalism:

- automatic status (by reason of position),
- power and authority conferred by position,
- expertise assumed because of position,
- embodiments of special status: dress, address and "perks,"
- protection of image (personal and institutional),

- resistance to critique,
- resistance to change,
- secrecy, and
- non-accountability.[17]

Each of these characteristics demonstrates and reinforces values, attitudes and practices. Each is worth consideration for its effects on ordained and lay alike.

The general consequences of clericalism are profound for all in the Church. It results ultimately in the loss of commitment to the holy and humble aspects of the priestly. The notion of the common priesthood of all the baptized is corrupted. Finally, there is loss of touch with both the vocational call and with those whom they are called to serve. It is clear that

> Clericalism … is always dysfunctional and haughty, crippling the spiritual and emotional maturity of the priest, bishop, or deacon caught in its web. Clericalism may command a superficial deference, but it blocks honest human communication and ultimately leaves the cleric practicing it isolated.[18]

This may be the main reason for the apparent lack of emotion and frequent callousness with which so many bishops responded to the crisis, as noted in Chapter 2.

Most priests enter the seminary not for power and prestige, but to serve the People of God. They enter it, for the most part, to build a community of prayer, worship, community and justice. Yet many of them are absorbed into this clerical culture with its frequent manifestations of clericalism. Fr. Michael Papesh highlights the profound effects of clericalism on priests through naming a set of contradictions priests live. Priests, he says, are formed inside clerical culture for responsibility outside it; promised to celibacy, but ill-equipped to live it; accountable within clerical culture for ministry outside it; both dependent and independent; shepherds of the flock and CEOs; highly circumscribed in ministry, yet broadly trusted; wanting relationships in ministry, but obliged to caution; community leaders, but personally lonely; ministers of unity in a fractured clerical culture; called to simplicity, but living in privilege; and moral authorities in public but privately "winking" at infidelity and indiscretions. So while status and "being on a pedestal" appears to make priests untouchable and superior, this creates enormous pressure on the ordinary men who are our priests.[19]

Most well-meaning laity put priests on pedestals and sustain them there. Many still want to keep them there because in some ways it relieves the burden of being fully involved in the life and ministry of the Church. The major consequence of clericalism for the laity is passivity and dependence. It has been said that:

> Lay clericalism is grounded in an immature dependence on clergy to mediate the believer's spirituality and relationship with God ... Lay clericalism enables the privileges and arrogance of the priesthood, trading adult negotiation of spirituality for ongoing clerical patronage/patronization.[20]

On the one hand, clericalism distorts and wounds the ordained; on the other, it disrespects and disempowers the laity. That is why parents refused to believe their children about what Father did to them. Parents who believed and who worked up the courage to go to the pastor or bishop to express their horror and anguish at what their child told them about a priest accepted that the matter would be dealt with, even when that meant seeing the offending priest moved from their parish to another. Sometimes they breathed a sigh of relief that their children were safe, even when others were at risk, and assumed no more responsibility.

Empirical and scientific research and individual experience demonstrate that all sexual abuse is fundamentally a misuse of power:

> this whole sexual crisis is deeply linked with power and the way in which power works in the Church at all levels, from the Vatican to the parish sacristan. It is not the power of Jesus who was gentle and lowly of heart. Every human institution revolves around the use of power ... The Church, alas, has often been infected by this same culture of control.[21]

We need to reflect carefully on this "culture of control," putting us at risk for unhealthy and unholy activities and choices.

Many observers of the clergy abuse crisis, notably the National Review Board of the United States Conference of Catholic Bishops, have noted a causal relationship between clericalism and sexual abuse on many levels, especially in the tendency of the hierarchy to protect priest-offenders, the tendency to secrecy, and massive denial of the magnitude of the problem.[22] Journalist Peter Steinfels identifies three factors about clericalism that fostered this denial and secrecy:

> First, priest abusers and their superiors operated within an enclosed, self-protective clerical culture ... Second, priests moved from assignment to assignment without the open process of inquiry, interview, and evaluation that was characteristic of many other religious groups as well as professional appointments. Third, a powerful aura of being consecrated surrounded the Catholic priesthood.[23]

The consequences for most bishops and the leadership of the Church in general are vividly demonstrated in the history: protection of the priest-offender, avoidance of scandal, and protection of image and institution took precedence for most over the calling to protection of the vulnerable, justice, and the humble acknowledgement of human frailty and sinfulness.

Clericalism's influence on the victims has also been identified: effects on the seduction and grooming for abuse on the victim's non-resistance (the trauma bond and religious duress) and the experience of prolonged abuse and failure to report it.[24] Victims' disbelief that a priest of God would do anything so wrong, coupled with intense fear of having somehow caused the abuse by tempting Father, and parental disbelief of the child and helplessness in the face of the power and authority of priests and bishops are also noted repeatedly in analyses of the crisis.

The majority of serious analyses of the abuse crisis have identified clericalism as a pervasive factor, particularly in its influence on secrecy and protection of image and institution. Clericalism distorts healthy and holy relationships and prevents proper participation of all the baptized in the life of the Church. It will have to be taken into account as we reflect on a prescription for healing the Church and finding new ways of mutual support and encouragement.

3. Gospel Themes that Propose an Alternative

Sexual abuse within the Church is a profound contradiction of the teaching and witness of Christ.—Pope John Paul II[25]

As you read of this history, what contradiction of the teaching and witness of Christ comes to mind? Which scriptures speak to you?

Some that have moved me follow:

- Jesus' response to titles that foster arrogance and suppress humility:

"But you are not to be called rabbi, for you have one teacher, and you are all students. And call no one your father on earth, for you have one Father – the one in heaven. Nor are you to be called instructors, for you have but one instructor, the Messiah." (Matthew 23:8-10)

- Jesus' total and all-encompassing humility:

Let the same mind be in you that was in Christ Jesus, who … emptied himself, taking the form of a slave… (Philippians 2:5-7)

- Jesus' rejection of superficial signs of respect and the need for adulation:

"They do all their deeds to be seen by others; for they make their phylacteries broad and their fringes long. They love to have the place of honour at banquets and the best seats in the synagogues, and to be greeted with respect in the marketplaces, and to have people call them rabbi." (Matthew 23:5)

- Jesus' modelling of the power and authority of servant-leadership:

[Jesus] got up from table, took off his outer robe, and tied a towel around himself. Then he poured water into a basin and began to wash the disciples' feet and to wipe them with the towel that was tied around him … After he had washed their feet, had put on his robe, and had returned to the table, he said to them, "Do you know what I have done to you? You call me Teacher and Lord – and you are right, for that is what I am. So if I, your Lord and Teacher, have washed your feet, you also ought to wash one another's feet. For I have set you as an example, so that you also should do as I have done to you." (John 13:4-5, 12-15)

- On the many gifts of the Spirit given to the whole Church:

Now there are varieties of gifts, but the same Spirit; and there are varieties of services, but the same Lord; and there are varieties of activities, but it is the same God who activates all of them in everyone. To each is given the manifestation of the Spirit for the common good. (1 Corinthians 12:4-7)

How does the Word speak to you?

_____

_____

_____

_____

> **4 SOME QUESTIONS FOR REFLECTION AND ACTION**
>
> - Is the issue of relationships and power in the Church an important one for you?
>
> - What is your experience of the use of power and authority in the Church?
>
> - Does the description of clericalism make sense to you?
>
> - What do you think are the effects of clericalism on priests, bishops and laity?
>
> - What are the consequences of clericalism on healthy relationships between ordained and laity?
>
> - Has the absence of women from the centre of Church activity influenced this crisis? If so, how?
>
> - What can you do to respond to the call of the Lord here?
>
> - What could your parish do?
>
> - What could your diocese do?

CHAPTER 5

FLESH AND BLOOD: MORAL THEOLOGY AND A THEOLOGY OF SEXUALITY

*God created humankind in his image,
in the image of God he created them;
male and female he created them. (Genesis 1:27)*

Jesus said to the crowds and to the disciples, "… do whatever [the scribes and the Pharisees] teach you and follow it; but do not do as they do, for they do not practice what they preach. They tie up heavy burdens, hard to bear, and lay them on the shoulders of others; but they themselves are unwilling to lift a finger to move them." (Matthew 23:1-3)

Sexuality is a beautiful, good, extremely powerful, sacred energy, given us by God and experienced in every cell of our being as an irrepressible urge to overcome our incompleteness, to move toward unity and consummation with that which is beyond us. —Fr. Ronald Rolheiser[1]

As we saw in Chapter 4, the first line of investigation of ill health generally assesses the anatomy and structural soundness of the body with the help of X-rays, diagnostic ultrasound and other technologies. But it is also necessary to assess a person's physiology and biochemistry, the active internal environment of the body. So we use studies such as blood and urine analysis to test the health of the fluids and forces that make us live and move and function.

Catholic teaching and beliefs around the body and sexuality are, in a sense, the life forces at work in the abuse crisis. They provide the focus and content for our response to the experience of human sexuality. While clergy sexual abuse of minors is primarily an issue of abuse of power, its particular manifestation lies in the complex and compelling area of human sexuality.

Objectives

In this chapter we will

1. review the experience of sexuality in the Catholic tradition;
2. analyze possible contributions from moral theology and the theology of sexuality to the clergy abuse crisis;
3. share some Gospel images of a prophetic alternative; and
4. propose some initial questions for reflection and discussion.

1 Sexuality in the Catholic Tradition

The sexual abuse of children and youth has become the only socially recognized sexual sin. Yet modern society is awash in sexual exploitation and violence, especially towards women and children. While society expresses public horror at the sexual abuse of children and youth, pornography – including child pornography – is rampant, and TV and movies are replete with themes where sexual manipulation and exploitation are standard fare. Prostitution and human trafficking are worldwide phenomena. It is precisely in this area of sexual morality where modern society is desperately in need of the Gospel witness of justice, compassion, tenderness and mercy – and where the Church has lost credibility. Yet Catholicism is known for its strict and centrally placed teaching on sexual morality. The sexual abuse of children and youth by clergy, and the associated institutional cover-ups and mismanagement, have contributed mightily to this loss of credibility and have raised some important questions about the Catholic experience of sexuality and the Church's moral teaching.

On the one hand, Catholics often experience the preaching of an impossibly ideal set of magisterial statements on marriage and sexuality. On the other hand, many Catholics have a general perception of sexuality as "dirty," secret and sinful. Catholics influenced by the Second Vatican Council experienced new and powerful teaching regarding the gift of human sexuality, especially in the married state. But for most, Catholic moral teaching has been dominated by rules and prohibitions regarding sexual and reproductive issues. As a result, many Catholics have experienced the Church as laying heavy burdens in the area of sexual behaviour: for example, the mother of seven with a husband who demands sex and who can't use artificial contraception, the use of condoms in HIV prevention in Africa, and infertile couples desperately desiring children but having limited use of modern medical technology to assist them. In a deep sense, teachings about sexuality and forgiveness for sexual sins are experienced as issues of power and control, not as the reconciling mercy of Jesus Christ. Theologian Yves Congar is reported to have said that "In the Catholic Church, it has often seemed that the sin of the flesh was the only sin, and obedience the only virtue." Of the seven deadly sins, lust is the one most people hear preached from pulpit.

At the core of the abuse crisis is a "problematic nexus around sexuality, power and the relationship between them."[2] In this chapter, we turn to an investigation of the theology of the body and sexuality for clues about its possible contribution to the shape, scope and duration of the crisis.

The early tradition

For all of Catholicism's focus on sexual morality, Jesus himself had little to say about it. Arguably, the most compelling story that comes to mind when we think of the Gospel and sexuality is that of Jesus and the woman taken in adultery (John 8:3-11). There, it is Jesus' enormous sensitivity and compassion to the woman that impresses and comforts.

Even in affirming the Old Testament prohibition on divorce (Matthew 19:3-9), Jesus grants an exception in the case of sexual morality, demonstrating his understanding of the gap between the ideal and lived human experience.

In general, the Christian scriptures demonstrate considerable ambiguity and contradiction regarding human bodies and sexuality. The New Testament is very concerned with the body and bodily integrity. The Incarnation of Jesus Christ is a central mystery of faith because "The Word became flesh and lived among us" (John 1:14). In and through his humanity, all flesh becomes holy. In the writings of St. Paul, the dignity of the body is emphasized: "always carrying in the body the death of Jesus, so that the life of Jesus may also be made visible in our bodies" (2 Corinthians 4:10). We understand the body as "a temple of the Holy Spirit." (1 Corinthians 6:19)

At the same time, the physical body can be controlled by the flesh – that is, by the sinful impulses of the body. Different authors of Scripture used the body and the flesh in different ways, so that confusion developed early regarding the *holy body* and the *sinful flesh*. From the beginnings of the life of the Church, sexual sins have had a special significance, as shown in the command to

> Shun fornication! Every sin that a person commits is outside the body; but the fornicator sins against the body itself. Or do you not know that your body is a temple of the Holy Spirit within you, which you have from God, and that you are not your own? For you were bought with a price; therefore glorify God in your body. (1 Corinthians 6:18-20)

The early Church's belief that the Second Coming was imminent and that all should prepare for it by abstaining from sex, because "when they rise from the dead, they neither marry nor are given in marriage" (Mark 12:25) continues to influence us today.

As we saw in Chapter 4, notions of cultic purity required the married priests of the time to refrain from sexual activity before celebrating the Eucharist. Celibacy was the higher state; celibates were understood to be holier than married persons, for

> The unmarried man is anxious about the affairs of the Lord, how to please the Lord; but the married man is anxious about the affairs of this world, how to please his wife, and his interests are divided. And the unmarried woman and the virgin are anxious about the affairs of the Lord, so that they may be holy in body and spirit; but the married woman is anxious about the affairs of the world, how to please her husband. (1 Corinthians 7:32-34)

From the second century onward, Church authorities disparaged sex as dirty, sinful and even unnatural. Marital sex was considered a necessary evil, a remedy for lust. St. Ambrose (339–397), a Father of the Church, considered sex part of the sinful world: "Virginity was the goal of all believers in imitation of Christ who, Ambrose taught, had never been touched by physical desire. He linked women to sexual temptation that ultimately led to sin and death."[3]

In the third century, Origen (184–253) and others developed an early dualism that emphasized the gap between body and soul and posited an active war between them.[4] As a result, from late antiquity in Western Christianity there arose a fear of primal drives located in the body, because these are a source of sin. These fears were captured in the teachings regarding the seven deadly sins. The spiritual soul is imprisoned in the physical body. The notion of a battle with the body underlies much of Christian asceticism. Flagellation, mortification and fasting were practices aimed at taming the body and its physical, especially lustful, desires for the life of the soul. Manichean and Gnostic heresies, which taught that the body/flesh was evil, were ultimately condemned, but their influence has lingered on in attitudes and pious practices in Catholicism.

St. Jerome (342–420) taught that the body must be controlled; Christians must avoid sexual attraction. A husband who loves his wife too much is guilty of adultery! St. Augustine (354–435), who had an active sex life before his conversion, for centuries set the tone for Catholicism's negative views on sexual desire. He held that sex is a good and useful force in human life but is debased by sin and passion. So sex is justifiable for human reproduction, but is evil if sought for other reasons. Theologian Cristina Traina concludes that "Augustine's belief that even 'good' marital sex ought to be hidden away … has probably contributed more than anything else to the impression that our sexuality is essentially private."[5] Augustine taught that the Fall of Adam and Eve proceeded from the couple's failure to deal with sexual desire, and that this is the core obstacle to holiness. Consequently, the Church needed to regulate tightly human sexuality.

Not surprisingly, then, in the medieval period, the Church developed a penitential code to be used by confessors to determine the seriousness of sins. St. Thomas Aquinas (1225–1274) was the first to suggest that sexual desire was natural and could be good as long as it was guided by reason and not experienced as pleasurable. Applying notions of natural law, he also categorized sexual sins as those in accord with nature and those contrary to nature. So, adultery and incest were seen as less sinful than masturbation and homosexuality because adultery and incest were open to procreation, and masturbation and homosexuality were not.

This set of beliefs and teachings strongly shaped the Catholic experience of the body, bodily pleasure and sexuality. The idea that sex could be an act of love and an essential aspect of marriage did not get much attention before the Second Vatican Council (1962–1965), with the work of theologians such as Bernard Häring. Pope John XXIII called the Second Vatican Council to prepare the Church for the modern world.[6] One major event requiring an urgent response was the development of birth control in 1960. Pope John created a Pontifical Commission for the Study of Population, Family and Births, known as the papal birth control commission, consisting of two physicians and four social scientists. Before it met for the first time, Pope John died. His successor, Pope Paul VI, confirmed the commission and over the next few years added 50 more members, many of them high-ranking clerics. In 1964, during the third session of the Council, just as it was to take up the issue of "responsible parenthood," Pope Paul VI removed birth control from the competence of the Council, indicating that it would be dealt with by the Pontifical Commission. He also forbade discussion of priestly celibacy. Both issues had been highly anticipated topics by clergy and lay Catholics around the world.

In contrast to the Council, which was the official assembly of Church leaders worldwide and held its deliberations before a wide variety of experts and shared collective responsibility for the work of the Council, the Pontifical Commission included laity and married members, worked diligently but in secret, and functioned as advisors to papal authority.[7] In 1968, Pope Paul wrote *Humanae Vitae*.[8] The encyclical rejected the majority report of the Pope's own commission and continued the ban on artificial means of birth control. The responses to the encyclical resulted in an ongoing and bitter polarization of the Church. Since the widespread failure of reception of the *Humanae Vitae* decision on contraception, there has been a gap between the Church's teaching and the practice of most Catholics in the area of contraception. This non-reception has had serious corrosive effects. For many Catholics, these effects shaped a culture within the Church where the activity of many members is in conflict with the formal teaching.

Certainly, there are Catholics who adhere to the Church teaching on birth control and the use of natural family planning. They experience it as positive and even compatible with feminist notions of controlling bodies as a crucial component of controlling lives. But many ordinary Catholics still thirst for a faith-based, relational understanding of the body and of human sexuality and for practical guidance for living as sexually active adults in today's world.

The Catholic experience of the body and sexuality has been characterized by some very clear features:

- ambivalence and confusion regarding the nature of human sexuality: sex is sacred but sex is sinful;
- sex is secret and not to be spoken about;
- sexual activity, by its very nature, must be linked to marriage between a man and a woman, and a covenantal commitment that is all-embracing and permanent;
- all sexual sins are intrinsically evil, particularly contraception, abortion and masturbation, permitting of no assessment of degree;
- celibacy is holier than the married state, but a fundamental image is that of Christ as Bridegroom to the Church;
- homosexuality is "intrinsically disordered," but a higher number of Catholic priests than in the general population are homosexual and they live in an all-male culture;
- the Catholic tradition makes much of the complementarity of men and women, but it is emphasized only in the physical sense of male–female intercourse.
- the experience of women is of segregation and subjugation, not collaboration and mutuality; their experiences are validated in terms of the male standard.

Attitudes that privileged celibacy over marriage and created an aura of control, secrecy and negativity regarding human sexuality have shaped Catholic thought and life. The result, especially in the pre-1960s era, when weekly confession was the norm, was a tradition that had Catholics thinking about sexual sin frequently and recounting transgressions in detail in the confessional to men who had little or no experience of the acts described.

This lived Catholic experience of sexuality, together with the disappointment and dissension surrounding *Humane Vitae*'s continued prohibition of artificial birth control, shaped the response of clergy and laity to the modern sexual abuse crisis in the Church.

2 Moral Theology and a Theology of Sexuality

Serious theological reflections on the clergy abuse crisis have raised important questions about the possible role of an inadequate legalistic understanding of morality and an inadequate theology of sexuality in the clergy abuse crisis.[9] Moral theology – distinct from dogmatic theology, which attends to the truths of faith about God and God's works – is a discipline that was created at the end of the sixteenth century. It is historically related to the medieval penitential books, which were developed to prepare senior seminarians for administering the Sacrament of Penance, fostering the notion that sexual matters are to be dealt with in secret. Richard McCormick describes this moral theology as sin-centred, confession-oriented and seminary-controlled.[10] This sin-centred science of the moral life, which was developed with no attention to Scripture or to virtue ethics, shaped the way in which the moral life was understood in the Church. This life was one of obedience to the commandments and to the canon law of the Church. This was the approach to the moral life, understood as a series of individual willed acts with no attention to the direct personal or communal consequences of the acts, in which priests were formed.

Well before Vatican II, the inadequacies of this understanding were evident to many. From the 1950s on there had been some evolution of moral theology and sexual ethics, mainly through the pioneering work of Bernard Häring, who notes that

> Moral theology, as I understand it, is not concerned first with decision making and discrete acts. Its basic task and purpose is to gain the right vision, to assess the main perspectives, and to present those truths and values which should bear upon decisions to be taken before God.[11]

The opening words of the foreword to Häring's *The Law of Christ* were clear in their focus – not on individual acts of men and women, but on the Lord: "the principle, the norm, the centre, and the goal of Christian moral theology is Christ."[12] Importantly, Häring recognized that an adequate moral theology of human sexuality required an authentic theology of sexuality.

Vatican II attempted a restoration of the theological focus on the whole of the Christian moral life that integrated moral theology with Scripture, spirituality and theology.

Pope John Paul II, in a valiant effort to return issues of sexuality to the context of love, began his systematic response to what he saw as the pastoral and catechetical failure of *Humanae Vitae* in a series of 130 fifteen-minute conferences at papal audiences between September 5, 1979, and November 28, 1984. These were brought together under the title *The Theology of the Body: Human Love in the Divine Plan*.[13] The Pope sought to change the tradition's suspicion of the body. His work, however, is dense and difficult to read. Some authors have attempted explanation.[14] This work has met with some enthusiasm, especially from younger Catholics who are searching for authenticity and a story of what authentic sexual relationships look like.[15]

However, there are many concerns regarding the adequacy of his approach and analysis. One prominent reviewer identified the Pope's work as a "disembodied theology of the body"[16] because it inadequately attends to the messiness of bodies and sex itself. The writer points out that reducing a theology of the body to sexuality and limiting sexuality to intercourse is fundamentally flawed. It must acknowledge all the other ways in which human embodiedness enables and limits human freedom. His final comment is this:

> John Paul II thinks of himself as doing "phenomenology", but never seems to look at actual human experience. Instead, he dwells on the nuances of words in biblical narratives and declarations, while fantasizing an ethereal and all-encompassing mode of mutual donation between man and woman that lacks any of the messy, clumsy, awkward, charming, casual, and, yes, silly aspects of love in the flesh. Carnality, it is good to remember, is at least as much a matter of humour as solemnity. In the pope's formulations, human sexuality is observed by telescope from a distant planet.[17]

But surely an elderly, male, celibate, holy man can only view married sexuality from afar. This reality raises important questions about who develops moral theology, particularly in the area of human sexuality.

Any adequate theology of sexuality must take into account the sexuality of all – celibate and married, clergy and laity.[18] A theology of sexuality for celibates is essential. Fr. Ron Rolheiser speaks to the power of human sexuality, the power to participate with God in the creation of life. He places healthy sexuality at the centre of the spiritual life:

> A healthy sexuality is the single most powerful vehicle there is to lead us to selflessness and joy, just as unhealthy sexuality helps constellate selfishness and unhappiness as does nothing else. We will be happy in this life, depending upon whether or not we have a healthy sexuality.[19]

This notion is not easily found in the Catholic tradition.

Sexuality and the abuse crisis

The Vatican position, that every question about human sexuality is settled and beyond discussion – that all sexual sins are intrinsically evil – and the faithful need only to obey, has profound implications for the notion of moral responsibility. It removes one of the most highly moral dimensions of life from scrutiny, deliberation and prayerful decision. It is in contradiction to modern notions of morality, which focus on Scripture and conscience formation and attend to the personal and communal consequences of actions.[20]

It is Church teaching that all sexual sins are intrinsically evil, particularly contraception, abortion and masturbation, but the sexual abuse of children and youth is a grave moral evil. Our inability to discuss what happened; the focus on the sins of the offenders; the failure to recognize the profoundly negative consequences of the abuse for the victim-survivors and for the Church – all these aspects appear rooted in an inadequate moral theology and an incomplete understanding of sexuality as well as in a tradition of not talking about sexual matters. As Fr. Norbert Rigali has noted,

> The moral perceptions and discernments of Church authorities with regard to the sexual abuse of children by priests, then, reflected not only moral theology's inadequate conception of Christian morality and of sin but also the discipline's inadequate treatment of human sexuality and the Church's lack of a adequate theology of human sexuality.[21]

This area requires response from the magisterium of the Church leadership, but we must all ask ourselves some important questions about how we consider and understand the gift of sexuality and sexual morality in our day-to-day lives.

3. Gospel Themes that Propose an Alternative

Sexual abuse within the Church is a profound contradiction of the teaching and witness of Christ.—Pope John Paul II[22]

As you read of this history, what contradiction of the teaching and witness of Christ comes to mind? Which scriptures speak to you?

Some that have moved me follow:

- On the importance of our bodies:

… always carrying in the body the death of Jesus, so that the life of Jesus may also be made visible in our bodies. (2 Corinthians 4:10)

- On Jesus' demands:

"For my yoke is easy, and my burden is light." (Matthew 11:30)

- On the mercy and love of Jesus:

"Teacher, this woman was caught in the very act of committing adultery. Now in the law Moses commanded us to stone such women. Now what do you say?" [Jesus] straightened up and said to her, "Woman, where are they? Has no one condemned you?" She said, "No one, sir." And Jesus said, "Neither do I condemn you. Go your way, and from now on do not sin again." (John 8:4-11)

How does the Word speak to you?

_____

_____

_____

_____

SOME QUESTIONS FOR REFLECTION AND ACTION

- Do you think that the Catholic experience and understanding of sex has played a role in this crisis?

- Has the understanding of morality as a set of rules rather than formation of persons into the mind of Christ abetted the situation?

- Have the background issues of sexual morality, where there has been a lack of reception of Church teaching by the general faithful, shaped the abuse crisis?

- Acknowledging that celibacy is not a causative factor in sex abuse, has celibacy nonetheless played a role?

- Recognizing that sexual abuse of children is almost exclusively a male phenomenon, has the exclusion of women from the centre of Church life and the development of morality contributed to the crisis?

- What can you do to respond to the call of the Lord here?

- What could your parish do?

- What could your diocese do?

CHAPTER 6

PRESCRIPTION: A RE-EVANGELIZATION OF THE CHURCH

Yet even now, says the Lord, return to me with all your heart, with fasting, with weeping, and with mourning; rend your hearts and not your clothing. (Joel 2:12)

Jesus said, "Those who are well have no need of a physician, but those who are sick." (Matthew 9:12)

As His Holiness has often observed, healing for victims must be of paramount concern in the Christian community, and it must go hand in hand with a profound renewal of the Church at every level.—Cardinal Tarcisio Bertone[1]

After assessing the patient's symptoms, obtaining the history and investigating the most likely and most serious causes, the doctor makes a judgment about the definitive diagnosis and moves to provide recommendations for treatment.

Everyone wants a quick and easy treatment. Today, drugs and interventions are demanded; we want instant relief for our distress and disease. After all, TV abounds with medical shows where there are miracle cures and where patients who collapse are resuscitated with the full technology of medicine in the first fifteen minutes of the episode; they suddenly return to a normal heartbeat, sit up and start talking. The episode usually ends with the fully recovered patient walking out the door to some great adventure. We all know it's not really like that, even when medicine does wonderful things. Healing is hard work and it takes time.

Often, the prescribed pills or recommended surgery are only one component of treatment. Full recovery and effective prevention of a relapse or recurrence may require a whole new way of life. Pills are easy to take; a lifestyle change is more difficult. We all like to think or hope that there must be an easier way.

Our reflections have clearly demonstrated that diagnosing root causes of the pain and suffering of the Body of Christ resulting from the abuse crisis is no easy matter. This is a complex, long-standing and multi-faceted disease. There is no single, simple spiritual pill or surgical procedure that will work here.

Objectives

In this final reflection we will

1. review what we have learned about the state of health of the Church in and through this crisis;
2. propose some essential elements in any effective prescription and identify who receives it;
3. share some Gospel images of a prophetic alternative; and
4. suggest some initial questions for reflection and discussion.

1. The Health of the Church

Asking about the health and holiness of the Church may be shocking to some. After all, we believe that the Church is one, *holy*, catholic and apostolic. While some make clear distinctions between different understandings of the Church, particularly separating the institution from communion, sacrament, herald, servant work for justice and the community of disciples,[2] in reality all these models are essential to understanding the mystery of the Church. While the Church is holy, not all members are holy; not all structures and practices and policies foster holiness.

Our history, examination of the experienced pain and suffering, and preliminary investigations earlier in this resource reveal a seriously traumatized and debilitated Church in need of urgent attention. The problem is a long-standing one, with many internal risk factors and environmental precipitants. Despite recent severe, widespread and very public exacerbation of pain and suffering, there is still, for many ordained and laity, an ongoing denial of the severity and urgency of the situation. Despite the overwhelming preponderance of evidence, some people still believe that the institutional Church and its organization and governance are basically sound, and that any pain and suffering we are experiencing are the result of sins and failures of individuals.

Our investigations and prayerful reflection suggest the primary diagnosis is that we have all been afflicted with a way of thinking and acting in "profound contradiction of the teaching and witness of Christ," as Pope John Paul II put it.³ The essential goal of treatment, then, must be a return to the mind and ways of Jesus, a re-evangelization of the Church itself.

Pope Benedict has called for a New Evangelization, especially of formerly Catholic/Christian nations in the West. He has appealed for "[T]he courage to forge new paths in responding to the changing circumstances and conditions facing the Church in her call to proclaim and live the Gospel today."⁴

This call, made nearly 50 years since the last invitation to renewal in the Second Vatican Council, is timely. The world and the Church have changed profoundly in the intervening years. However, a careful review of the crisis of sexual abuse by clergy and religious demonstrates clearly that the Church cannot be a sign of the *Good News* unless and until it deals effectively with the decades of bad news regarding the violation of children and youth by priests and tackles the underlying systemic and cultural issues that fostered the crisis. The now debilitated Church will not have the energy and strength for the "new ardour, new methods, new expressions" of the New Evangelization, so desperately needed, until it, too, is purified and renewed.

What have our initial investigations revealed? What have our prayerful, careful reflections on the pain and suffering and history of this crisis revealed that might help us identify crucial elements in any prescriptions for healing?

What we have learned from our examination of our patient, the Church, the history of the problem, and the efficacy of treatments tried thus far:

- Serious and long-standing abuse of some of the most vulnerable members of the family of the faith – children and youth – has happened.
- The abuse has been of both a sexual and spiritual nature. Many priests consciously used the power of their spiritual status in the abuse, and frequently used spiritual and religious justifications for their acts, committing blasphemy and sacrilege.
- The lifelong consequences of the abuse are, for most victim-survivors, serious. These include physical, psychological and religious/spiritual elements. The most serious consequence is the inability of some victim-survivors to believe and trust in a merciful, loving God.
- The sexual abuse of children and youth was committed by both pathological sexual predators and by weak, sexually confused and conflicted men, with the latter usually in situations of isolation, loneliness and alcohol abuse. This distinction is crucial for our appropriate response.

- Most priest-offenders, though called "Father," had little or no direct knowledge and experience of fathering or of the needs of children and youth.
- While the focus today is on children and youth, the abuse of women and the psychological abuse of men and women in the Church are important related issues.
- The response of ordinary Catholics to the victim-survivors is ambivalent and at times has revictimized them.
- Our response to the abusers presents important challenges to our foundational notions of forgiveness.
- Healing and reconciliation are crucial, complex issues for
    - individual victim-survivors, some of whom want nothing to do with reconciliation, and others who need healing and reconciliation with the community, and
    - those Catholics for whom this issue was the last straw in their frustration with the Church.

The Church leadership's response to the reports of abuse of individuals, with a few recent exceptions, was consistent across time and cultures. It has been characterized by

- denial and minimization of the nature and severity of the harm done;
- insensitivity and apparent callous indifference to the pain and suffering of the victim-survivors and their families;
- protection of the priest offenders, above and beyond any obligation to due process and duty to protect the rights of the priest;
- action to avoid scandal, where the scandal was understood to revolve around the reputation of the priest and Church, not the harm done to the innocent;
- the widespread use of secrecy in managing the issue;
- failure of bishops and religious superiors to enforce applicable canon law, dramatically demonstrating accountability in the Church as only vertical – priest to bishop; bishop to Rome – with no required accountability to the faithful nor even to policies and protocols developed by national episcopal conferences;
- lack of a generally accepted code of professional ethics for priests who judge and advise on the ethical and moral behaviour of others; and
- focus on protocols to deal with individual allegations and preventive policies, such as improved seminary formation and safe ministry environments.

Many within the Church, and from a variety of disciplines outside the Church, have tried to understand the essential nature of the abuse crisis. They have identified important elements and proposed a variety of remedies:

- Most serious reflection and analysis of the issue agree that there are two separate but related crises operative here:
  - the direct abuse of individual children and youth by clergy and religious, and
  - the lack of pastoral response and appropriate management by Church leadership.
- Each of the different understandings of the nature of the crisis – authority, fidelity, lust and sexuality, patriarchy, trust, and abuse of power, specifically in clericalism – raises important considerations. None, taken alone, captures the complexity of the crisis.
- In part, these different understandings are a reflection of divisions within the Church. Some have used the crisis to advance pre-set liberal or conservative agendas.
- Essentially, there are two different primary diagnoses:
  - the Church is in good health; this is all about individual sins and failings; the treatment is clarity, orthodoxy, obedience and compliance with protocols and policies; and
  - the Church itself is in need of purification and renewal and treatment for some cultural and systemic pathology.

Three issues emerge from our investigations that require particular attention: clericalism, sexuality and Church leadership.

Clericalism

Clericalism, the particular manifestation of abuse of power that facilitated this crisis,

- is concerned with protection of the particular interests, power and privilege of the clergy and is characterized by an authoritarian style of ministerial leadership, a rigidly hierarchical worldview, and a virtual identification of the holiness and grace of the Church with the clerical state and thereby with clerics;[5]
- corrupts the holy for ordained and lay alike;[6]
- drives a wedge between clergy and laity and prevents the recognition of the mutual need of ordained and lay that requires new ways of mutual support;
- exacerbates divisions across priests who have differing theologies of the priesthood[7] and differing ecclesiologies (e.g., Vatican II priests, John Paul II priests, millennial priests);
- fosters non-involvement and the impotence of the laity;
- develops a culture incapable of assessing its own negative biases;

- ultimately distorts the call to ordained priesthood and puts those infected out of touch with those whom they have been called to serve.

Sexuality and morality

The crisis has occurred in the context of the Catholic experience of the body and sexuality, shaped by

- ambivalent views of the body and human sexuality;
- a conviction that sex is secret, not to be spoken about;
- a moral theology developed to judge individual sins, especially sexual sins;
- a culture of controlling human sexuality, understood as an obstacle to holiness; and
- an inadequate theology of the body and sexuality;
- a failure to confront the difficulty of living celibacy in the priesthood.

Church leadership

Leadership has consistently focused on individual sins and crimes rather than on the systemic and cultural factors that have shaped the response of Church leaders:

- priority has been given to policies, protocols and prevention;
- deeper issues, including some theological and structural ones, have not been addressed;
- the Church has been judged to be basically in good health. The current crisis is the fault of individuals. The obvious prescription is clear rules and strict enforcement.

② Elements in Any Effective Prescription

The effectiveness of any prescription depends on an accurate diagnosis and assessment of underlying causes and risk factors, the appropriate treatment, a compliant patient who trusts the diagnosis and has faith in the prescription, and an abundance of grace.

The primary diagnosis here seems clear: "Sexual abuse within the Church is a profound contradiction of the teaching and witness of Christ."[8]

The elements of any effective remedy are then also clear and radical:

- Let the same mind be in you that was in Christ Jesus (Philippians 2:1-8)
- "… learn from me; for I am gentle and humble in heart" (Matthew 11:29)

Any prescription for the healing of the Church must model itself on the healing and reconciling mission of Jesus himself. His cures all contained three elements: response to the felt pain, suffering and dysfunction of the person; restoration of the person's sense of wholeness and holiness; and a reintegration of the person into the community, which is then challenged to respond with justice and compassion. This is a lifestyle change of the greatest magnitude!

We need to write the prescription together and to recognize some essential elements in any effective treatment.

Urgent Rx for all in the Church

- **We need to stop denying the pain and suffering in this crisis and acknowledge our weakness, sinfulness and need for God's mercy.**
- **We need to develop new ways of openness, sharing and meaningful discourse in the Church, which includes ordained and lay, men and women, young and old, "liberals" and "conservatives."**
- **We need to acknowledge our moral and structural blindness to violence, injustice and exploitation of the vulnerable in our midst and commit to restorative justice and right relations in the Church.**
- **We need to accept that the call to transformation, renewal and holiness is for all.**

Therefore in the Church, everyone whether belonging to the hierarchy, or being cared for by it, is called to holiness … [T]his holiness of the Church is unceasingly manifested, and must be manifested, in the fruits of grace which the Spirit produces in the faithful; it is expressed in many ways in individuals, who in their walk of life, tend toward the perfection of charity, thus causing the edification of others…Thus it is evident to everyone, that all the faithful of Christ of whatever rank or status, are called to the fullness of the Christian life and to the perfection of charity; by this holiness as such a more human manner of living is promoted in this earthly society.[9]

Long-term lifestyle changes

In the deepest sense, the Church needs a change of lifestyle if we are to be the sign and sacrament of the Reign of God in our world.

- **We must reclaim our foundational identity as the one priesthood of Christ in which all the baptized share.**[10]

At the centre of all priesthood is self-giving, a recognition of the need for the sanctification of all life, and a commitment to live in ways that manifest God's love and justice.

The Christian community priests when its members take on the mind and heart of Jesus; when they show forth singleness of purpose in their following of the risen Lord; when their daily lives are an expression of praise and gratitude – and joyous song – to the One Jesus called "Father": when they identify compassionately with the broken and disposed of society; when they relate personally to others as peers, as brothers and sisters; and when they use the power of their voice to speak out and act for the rights of the voiceless. More simply, the community priests when they love the Lord with their whole heart and their whole mind and their whole soul, and their neighbour, even their enemy, as themselves.[11]

- **Individually and collectively we need to re-establish the essential link between Eucharist and ministry.**

- **We need a revitalized understanding of our real need for God's mercy, the centrality of forgiveness of our sins and the Sacrament of Reconciliation.**

- **We must work together to establish relationships in the Church that reflect the reality of our "mutual need" as ordained and lay, men and women.**

The Church requires a real, active experience of interdependence "since pastors and the other faithful are bound to each other by a mutual need."[12] The centrality of "mutual interdependence" and "mutual need" presents a vision of Church as priestly people with roles and responsibilities determined in relation to each other. It commits us to new ways of mutual support in the complex, demanding and sometimes hostile world of today.

- **We must all commit to continuing adult formation in the faith that is rooted in Scripture and in the formation of conscience.**

Rx for Church leadership

While this is primarily a spiritual crisis for all in the Church, it also demonstrates the need for reform of some cultural and systemic issues. While all can participate in a process of spiritual conversion, only Church leaders can facilitate the development of policies and structures that can promote and sustain the conversion and purification.

Clericalism fostered the abuse of power in this crisis and is in deep contradiction with the proper understanding of priesthood, especially as confirmed in *Lumen Gentium* and *Christifideles Laici*.[13]

- **Leadership must accept the corrosive effects of clericalism on ordained and lay and conform the use of power and authority in the Church to the model of Jesus himself.**

- **Leadership must participate in the development and promotion of a culture of openness, transparency and dialogue.**

Pope John Paul II identified "the need today for each bishop to develop 'a pastoral style which is ever more open to collaboration with all', grounded in a clear understanding of the relationship between the ministerial priesthood and the common priesthood of the baptized."[14] This ecclesial communion also "presupposes the participation of every category of the faithful, inasmuch as they share responsibility for the good of the particular Church which they themselves form."[15]

- **Leadership must restore and renew a morality where "the principle, the norm, the centre, and the goal of Christian moral theology is Christ."[16]**
- **Church leadership must address some theological and structural issues in the light of our transformation with particular attention to mutuality, mandatory celibacy, the role of laity in the Church, the treatment of women in the Church, and sexual morality.**

Some wish to revise or eliminate structures as a first response to this crisis, but careful diagnosis shows that the need for renewal is deep, spiritual and personal and communal. Until this renewal is well under way, the debilitated Body of Christ will not have the vigour to develop structures that foster a renewal rooted in the mind of Christ.

Pope Benedict's call for a New Evangelization provides a powerful opportunity to link response to the clergy sexual abuse crisis within it. "As His Holiness has often observed, healing for victims must be of paramount concern in the Christian community, and it must go hand in hand with a profound renewal of the Church at every level."[17]

Are we ready to take our medicine and return to a healthy and holy lifestyle? The healing of the Church as a sign of the Kingdom of God in our world depends on it.

Gospel Themes that Propose an Alternative

Sexual abuse within the Church is a profound contradiction of the teaching and witness of Christ.—Pope John Paul II[18]

As you read of this history what contradiction of the teaching and witness of Christ comes to mind? Which scriptures speak to you?

Some that have moved me follow:

› On Jesus' compassion, mercy and desire to heal:

A leper came to [Jesus] begging him, and kneeling he said to him, "If you choose, you can make me clean." Moved with pity, Jesus stretched out his hand and touched him, and said to him, "I do choose. Be made clean!" Immediately the leprosy left him, and he was made clean. (Mark 1:40-43)

› On reclaiming our fundamental, baptismal identity:

You are a chosen race, a royal priesthood, a holy nation. (1 Peter 2:9)

› On true authority and power rooted in humble service to one another:

[Jesus] got up from table, took off his outer robe, and tied a towel around himself. Then he poured water into a basin and began to wash the disciples' feet and to wipe them with the towel that was tied around him … After he had washed their feet, had put on his robe, and had returned to the table, he said to them, "Do you know what I have done to you? You call me Teacher and Lord – and you are right, for that is what I am. So if I, your Lord and Teacher, have washed your feet, you also ought to wash one another's feet. For I have set you as an example, so that you also should do as I have done to you." (John 13:4-5, 12-15)

› On the gifts of all the community as essential:

Now there are varieties of gifts, but the same Spirit; and there are varieties of services, but the same Lord; and there are varieties of activities, but it is the same God who activates all of them in everyone. To each is given the manifestation of the Spirit for the common good. (1 Corinthians 12:4-7)

How does the Word speak to you?

_____

_____

_____

 SOME QUESTIONS FOR REFLECTION AND ACTION

- What is the most important thing you have learned from this reflection process?

- What do you think are the essential first steps in healing?

- From your experience, what are the biggest obstacles to an effective response to this crisis?

- Are you ready to commit personally to a new way of being as priest and people so as to be the faithful People of God we are called to be?

- Is your parish ready to commit to a new way of being as priest and people so as to be the faithful People of God we are called to be?

- Is your diocese ready to commit to a new way of being as bishop, priests and people so as to be the faithful People of God we are called to be?

- What attitudes, policies and structures need to change to support you in your commitment?

SOME THOUGHTS AND PRAYERS REGARDING PROGNOSIS

So if anyone is in Christ, there is a new creation: everything old has passed away; see, everything has become new! (2 Corinthians 5:17-18)

We must face the truth of the past; repent it; make good the damage done. And yet we must move forward day by day along the painful path of renewal, knowing that it is only when our human misery encounters face-to-face the liberating mercy of God that our Church will be truly restored and enriched.— Archbishop Diarmuid Martin[19]

The big question in the minds of patients and their loved ones are about recovery and future health and functioning. All are looking for a judgment of the outcome, the prognosis, of the illness, injury or disease. Prognosis is the most risky and difficult act of medicine. It requires a correct diagnosis, an appropriate prescription, a compliant patient who has the basic health to respond to the treatment, adequate resources to support the patient, and an abundance of grace. The prognosis could be full recovery, recovery with minor side effects, survival with lifelong consequences, or death.

Many assume that there will, in time, be a positive outcome from all this, because the Holy Spirit is with the Church. After all, we have endured for over 2,000 years and have had a long history of scandalous and sinful behaviour mixed with the holy, prophetic and courageous witness to justice and compassion. But the prognosis here is more fragile and more uncertain than we might imagine, because we must respond to that same Spirit.

In the Introduction, we noted Brueggemann's belief that in order for a community to generate the prophetic criticism and prophetic energizing that move us to the freedom of God and ways of justice, compassion and healing, the community needs at least four things:

- a long and available memory,
- a sense of pain and loss,
- the active practice of hope, and
- an effective mode of discourse.[20]

The Church certainly has a long memory. If we can remember our history of sin and need for God's mercy, and can accept our need to recall the words and witness of Jesus himself, we have a powerful vision of the way forward.

Surely, we are experiencing severe pain, suffering and loss. Our experience and the knowledge of the dire consequences of denial of the need for help should impel us to seek healing.

Hope is crucial, but it is not at all clear how real and active our practice of hope is today in the Church. Recall that hope is "The theological virtue by which we desire the kingdom of God and eternal life, place our trust in God's promises and rely not on our own strength but on the help of the grace of the Holy Spirit."[21] Many appear to have given up hope in the Church as a sign of the healing and reconciling ministry of Jesus Christ in our world.

Abandoning hope is the unforgivable sin. We must find ways to keep hope alive by doing what we can and opening ourselves to the call of the Holy Spirit.

The most problematic element in responding to this crisis is the lack of an effective mode of discourse. Catholics have had little practice in open, mutual, effective conversation about matters of faith and doubt. If we can learn to speak together about these difficult things, we can find ways of healing.

Despite these concerns, the possibility of the prophetic is alive and well if we but accept it, individually and as a Church. Individually and communally, we need to identify and confront inhibitors of transformation, especially the fear of the depth and breadth of transformation being called for! We must accept loving the Church in its sinfulness or not loving it at all.

The Body of Christ is hurting. If, despite our fears, we can begin together a process of purification and renewal, then the prognosis for healing and restoration of health is very good indeed. We have the Great Physician with us.

> "Lord, save us! We are perishing!" And Jesus said to them, "Why are you afraid, you of little faith?" (Matthew 8:24-25)

APPENDIX I

EARLY HISTORY OF SEXUAL ABUSE BY CLERGY

309	Council of Elvira – one half of its canons dealt with sexual transgressions, including condemning sex between adult men and young boys
533	The *Digest of Justinian* speaks to same-sex relations with young boys
8th century	The *Penitential of Bede* advises strict penalties for clerics who commit sodomy with children
1051	The *Book of Gomorrah* by St. Peter Damien contains an explicit outcry against clerical sexual contact with young boys
1139	Second Lateran Council mandates clerical celibacy
1140	*Decree of Gratian* contains a specific reference to sexual sins with young boys, *stuprum pueri*
1917	*Code of Canon Law* is promulgated
1983	Revised *Code of Canon Law* is published

APPENDIX II

SOME KEY MODERN HISTORY

1967 First public discussion in the US of clergy sexual abuse of minors at National Association for Pastoral Renewal meeting in Notre Dame, Indiana

1974 Fr. Barry Glendinning, an instructor at St. Peter's Seminary in London, Ontario, is convicted of six counts of gross indecency

1983 Fr. Gilbert Gauthe of Henry, Louisiana, is charged with eleven counts of child abuse; he pleads guilty and is sentenced to 20 years in prison

1985 Fr. Thomas Doyle, Fr. Mike Peterson and Ray Mouton prepare a report, *The Manual*, for the US bishops on the scope of the abuse crisis; it is never presented

1985 On June 7, the *National Catholic Reporter* publishes a consolidation of reports regarding clergy sex abuse from US, Canada and Ireland during the early 1980s

1988 First public statement, the USCC Pedophilia Statement, is published (*Origins* 17:624)

1988 Fr. James Hickey of St. John's, Newfoundland, is charged with 32 counts of sexual misconduct

1989 John Allen Loftus writes *Sexual Abuse in the Church*

1989 Archdiocesan Commission of Enquiry into the Sexual Abuse of Children by Members of the Clergy is established in St. John's, Newfoundland; it produces its report in 1990

1991 Cardinal Joseph Bernadin of Chicago appoints a commission to provide guidelines; it reports in July 1992

1992 Fr. James Porter, Fall River, Massachusetts, is arrested; he pleads guilty to 41 counts of sexual assault and goes to prison

1992	CCCB Ad Hoc Committee on Sexual Abuse produces two resources: *From Pain to Hope* and *Breach of Trust, Breach of Faith*
1992	USCCB's "5 Principles" are developed; first public statement by a USCCB President is made
1992	SNAP [Survivors Network of those Abused by Priests] Victim/Survivor Networks is established
1993	Archbishop Robert Sanchez of New Mexico resigns because of allegations regarding teenage girls
1993	First public statement is made by Pope John Paul II in a June Letter to the US bishops
1993	USCCB forms Ad Hoc Committee on Sexual Abuse, headed by Bishop John F. Kinney of Bismarck, North Dakota
1994	New *Catechism of the Catholic Church* is issued; contains a note regarding abuse
1995	Australian Bishops' "Pastoral Statement on Child Protection and Child Sexual Abuse" is published; by 2010, 71 priests and religious convicted
1997	Dallas jury awards a staggering $120 million to eleven victims, indicating they were disgusted with the way the Church kept Rudy Kos in ministry
2001	*Sacramentorium Sanctitatis Tutela*, Vatican procedural norms on dealing with clerical abuse, reserved to the Congregation for the Doctrine of the Faith (CDF)
2001	Catholic Bishops Conference of England and Wales publishes the *Nolan Report*
2002	The *Boston Globe* publishes a front-page story in January about the cover-up regarding John Geoghan and follow-up articles
2002	American Cardinals are summoned to Rome in April
2002	In June, the USCCB issues its *Charter for the Protection of Children and Young People*
2002	Cardinal Law resigns in mid-December
2004	Publication of *The Nature and Scope of Sexual Abuse of Minors by Catholic Priests and Deacons in the United States, 1950–2002*, by the John Jay College of Criminal Justice, Catholic Church
2006	Fr. Charles Sylvestre of London, Ontario, is convicted of 47 counts of indecent assault of girls; London ultimately has 22 priests convicted and charged
2009	Bishop Raymond Lahey of Antigonish, Nova Scotia, is arrested in September for possession and importation of child pornography

2009	Murphy and Ryan reports are published in Ireland
2010	Vatican revisions confirm the authority of the CDF to judge Cardinals, Patriarchs and bishops, and speeds up the canonical processes
2011	On Ash Wednesday, Philadelphia Grand Jury indicts a top official, Msgr. William Lynn, for mishandling cases of abuse; Cardinal Bevilaqua is criticized
2011	In May, the CDF issues a Circular Letter with "guidelines" to assist with dealing with cases of clergy sexual abuse
2011	In May, publication of *The Causes and Context of Sexual Abuse of Minors by Catholic Priests in the United States, 1950–2010* by the John Jay College of Criminal Justice
2011	On May 13, Amnesty International names the Vatican on human rights concerns for not sufficiently complying with international mandates, to which it is a signatory, protecting children from abuse
2011	In September, the Center for Constitutional Rights, on behalf of SNAP and five individual claimants, submits a request to the Prosecutor of the International Criminal Court
2011	In October, Bishop Robert Finn of the Diocese of Kansas City–St. Joseph is indicted by a county grand jury for failure to report suspected child abuse
2011	On December 16, Dutch Commission report is published
2012	On February 12, "Towards Healing and Renewal" Symposium is held in Rome
2012	In June, Monsignor William J. Lynn of the Archdiocese of Philadelphia was found guilty of child endangerment. He is the first senior Church official in the United States convicted for covering up sex abuse by clergy.

ENDNOTES

Preface

1 Catherine of Siena & Noffke S. 2000. *The Letters of Catherine of Siena*. Rev. ed. Tempe, AZ: Arizona Center for Medieval and Renaissance Studies.

2 Winter GA, Commission of Enquiry into the Sexual Abuse of Children by Members of the Clergy & Archdiocese of St. John's. 1990. *The Report of the Archdiocesan Commission of Enquiry into the Sexual Abuse of Children by Members of the Clergy – Volume I*. St. John's, NL: Archdiocese of St. John's, 91.

3 Hogan L. 2011. Clerical and Religious Child Abuse: Ireland and Beyond. *Theological Studies* 72(1):170–186.

4 Canadian Conference of Catholic Bishops Ad Hoc Committee on Child Sexual Abuse & Canadian Conference of Catholic Bishops. 1992. *From Pain to Hope: Report From the CCCB Ad Hoc Committee on Child Sexual Abuse*. Ottawa, ON: Canadian Conference of Catholic Bishops, 172.

5 Canadian Conference of Catholic Bishops Ad Hoc Committee on Child Sexual Abuse & Canadian Conference of Catholic Bishops. 1992. *Breach of Trust, Breach of Faith: Child Sexual Abuse in the Church and Society: Materials for Discussion Groups*. Ottawa, ON: Canadian Conference of Catholic Bishops.

6 Bernier R, Cere D, Kenny N, Padamadan S & Waind J. 2012. Trauma and Transformation: the Catholic Church and the Sexual Abuse Crisis. Conference Website and Posted Proceedings, McGill University, 14–15 October, 2011. McGill University Centre for Research on Religion. Available from: <http://traumaandtransformation.org/> (accessed 24 January 2012).

7 Archbishop Anthony Mancini. 2 October 2009. Letter to the Roman Catholic Faithful of Nova Scotia. Archdiocese of Halifax. Available from: <www.catholichalifax.org/images/stories/BishopOffice/2009 10 02 All RC of NS.pdf > (accessed 24 January 2012).

8 Pope Benedict XVI. 19 March 2010. Pastoral Letter of the Holy Father Pope Benedict XVI to the Catholics of Ireland. The Vatican. Available from: <http://www.vatican.va/holy_father/benedict_xvi/letters/2010/documents/hf_ben-xvi_let_20100319_church-ireland_en.html> (accessed 24 January 2012).

Introduction

1 Radcliffe (O.P.) T. 2010. Come to Me All You Who Labour. In: Littleton J & Maher E, editors. *The Dublin/Murphy Report: a Watershed for Irish Catholicism?* Dublin: Columba Press; pp.17–28 at 18.

2 John Jay College of Criminal Justice, Catholic Church & United States Conference of Catholic Bishops. 2004. *The Nature and Scope of Sexual Abuse of Minors by Catholic Priests and Deacons in the United

States, 1950–2002. Washington, DC: United States Conference of Catholic Bishops; John Jay College of Criminal Justice. 2011. *The Causes and Context of Sexual Abuse of Minors by Catholic Priests in the United States, 1950–2010.* Washington, DC: United States Conference of Catholic Bishops.

3. Lytton TD. 2008. *Holding Bishops Accountable: How Lawsuits Helped the Catholic Church Confront Clergy Sexual Abuse.* Cambridge, MA: Harvard University Press.

4. Higgins MW & Kavanagh P. 2010. *Suffer the Children Unto Me: an Open Inquiry into the Clerical Sex Abuse Scandal.* Toronto: Novalis.

5. Rigert J. 2008. *An Irish Tragedy: How Sex Abuse by Irish Priests Helped Cripple the Catholic Church.* Baltimore, MD: Crossland Press; Littleton J & Maher E. 2010. *The Dublin/Murphy Report: a Watershed for Irish Catholicism?* Dublin: Columba Press.

6. Brueggemann W. 2001. *The Prophetic Imagination.* 2nd ed. Minneapolis, MN: Augsburg Fortress, 11.

7. Brueggemann, *The Prophetic Imagination.* 2nd ed. Minneapolis, MN: Augsburg Fortress, 81.

8. Heschel AJ & Heschel S. 2001. *Moral Grandeur and Spiritual Audacity Essays.* 4th pbk. ed. New York, NY: Farrar, Straus & Giroux, 225.

9. Brueggemann, *The Prophetic Imagination.* 2nd ed. Minneapolis, MN: Augsburg Fortress.

10. Vella JK. 2002. *Learning to Listen, Learning to Teach: the Power of Dialogue in Educating Adults.* Rev. ed. San Francisco, CA: Jossey-Bass.

11. Pope Paul VI. 21 November 1964. Dogmatic Constitutions on the Church: *Lumen Gentium.* The Vatican. Available from: <http://www.vatican.va/archive/hist_councils/ii_vatican_council/documents/vat-ii_const_19641121_lumen-gentium_en.html> (accessed 24 January 2012).

Chapter 1

1. Pope John Paul II. 22 November 2001. Post-Synodal Apostolic Exhortation: *Ecclesia in Oceania.* The Vatican. Available from: <http://www.vatican.va/holy_father/john_paul_ii/apost_exhortations/documents/hf_jp-ii_exh_20011122_ecclesia-in-oceania_en.html> (accessed 24 January 2012).

2. Rosetti SJ. 1990. *A Tragic Grace: the Catholic Church and Child Sexual Abuse.* Collegeville, MN: Liturgical Press; Berry J. 2000. *Lead Us Not into Temptation: Catholic Priests and the Sexual Abuse of Children.* 1st Illinois paperback ed. Urbana, IL: University of Illinois Press; The Investigative Staff of the Boston Globe. 2002. *Betrayal: the Crisis in the Catholic Church.* Boston, MA: Little, Brown and Company; John Jay College of Criminal Justice, Catholic Church & United States Conference of Catholic Bishops. 2004. *The Nature and Scope of Sexual Abuse of Minors by Catholic Priests and Deacons in the United States, 1950–2002.* Washington, DC: United States Conference of Catholic Bishops; John Jay College of Criminal Justice. 2011. *The Causes and Context of Sexual Abuse of Minors by Catholic Priests in the United States, 1950–2010.* Washington, DC: United States Conference of Catholic Bishops; Podles LJ. 2008. *Sacrilege: Sexual Abuse in the Catholic Church.* Baltimore, MD: Crossland Press.

3. DeCosse D. 2007. Freedom of the Press and Catholic Social Thought. *Theological Studies* 68:865–899; Higgins MW & Kavanagh P. 2010. *Suffer the Children Unto Me: an Open Inquiry into the Clerical Sex Abuse Scandal.* Toronto: Novalis.

4. Lytton TD. 2008. *Holding Bishops Accountable: How Lawsuits Helped the Catholic Church Confront Clergy Sexual Abuse.* Cambridge, MA: Harvard University Press, 42.

5. Frawley-O'Dea MG. 2007. *Perversion of Power: Sexual Abuse in the Catholic Church.* 1st ed. Nashville, TN: Vanderbilt University Press; Frawley-O'Dea MG & Goldner V. 2007. *Predatory Priests, Silenced Victims: the Sexual Abuse Crisis and the Catholic Church.* Mahwah, NJ: The Analytic Press; Plante TG. 1999. *Bless Me Father for I Have Sinned: Perspectives on Sexual Abuse Committed by Roman Catholic Priests.* Westport, CT: Praeger.

6. Frawley-O'Dea, MG. 2007. *Perversion of Power: Sexual Abuse in the Catholic Church.* 1st ed. Nashville, TN: Vanderbilt University Press; Frawley-O'Dea MG & Goldner V. 2007. *Predatory Priests, Silenced Victims: the Sexual Abuse Crisis and the Catholic Church.* Mahwah, NJ: The Analytic Press.

7. McLaughlin BR. 1994. Devastated Spirituality: the Impact of Clergy Sexual Abuse on the Survivor's Relationship with God and the Church. *Sexual Addiction & Compulsivity* 1(2):145–158.

8. Rosetti SJ. 1990. *A Tragic Grace: the Catholic Church and Child Sexual Abuse.* Collegeville, MN: Liturgical Press.

9. Bergeron G. 2004. *Don't Call Me a Victim.* Lowell, MA: King Printing Company; Estrada H. 2011. *UnHoly Communion: Lessons Learned from Life Among Pedophiles, Predators, and Priests.* New Mexico: Red Rabbit Press; Fortune MM. 1999. *Is Nothing Sacred? The Story of a Pastor, the Women He Sexually Abused, and the Congregation He Nearly Destroyed.* Cleveland, OH: United Church Press; Galasso C. 2007. *Crosses: Portraits of Clergy Abuse.* London: Trolley Ltd.; Lembo T. 2007. *The Hopeville Fire Department: a Boy's Tale of Betrayal by One of New England's Most Notorious Priests.* Doylestown, PA: Prose & Pictures, Inc.; O'Gorman C. 2009. *Beyond Belief.* London: Hodder & Stoughton; Price D. 2008. *Altar Boy, Altered Life: a True Story of Sexual Abuse.* Indianapolis, IN: Dog Ear Publishing, LLC.

10. Cardinal Marc Ouellet. 7 February 2012. Homily for the Penitential Vigil on the Occasion of the Symposium "Towards Healing and Renewal," 1. Canadian Conference of Catholic Bishops. Available from: <http://www.cccb.ca/site/images/stories/pdf/Cardinal_Ouellet_Prayer_Service_Rome_2012.pdf> (accessed 3 March 2012).

11. Cere D. May 2010. Toward a Gospel Witness: Confronting Child Abuse. Homiletic and Pastoral Review, paragraph 22. Available from: <http://www.catholiceducation.org/articles/apologetics/ap0344.htm> (accessed 11 May 2011).

12. Myers JEB. 2006. *Child Protection in America: Past, Present, and Future.* Oxford & New York: Oxford University Press.

13. John Jay College of Criminal Justice, Catholic Church & United States Conference of Catholic Bishops. 2004. *The Nature and Scope of Sexual Abuse of Minors by Catholic Priests and Deacons in the United States, 1950–2002.* Washington, DC: United States Conference of Catholic Bishops.

14. Finkelhor D & Jones LM. January 2004. Explanations for the Decline in Child Sexual Abuse Cases. United States Department of Justice, Office of Justice Programs, Office of Juvenile Justice and Delinquency Prevention. Available from: <http://purl.access.gpo.gov/GPO/LPS44917>

15. Finkelhor D & Araji S. 1986. *A Sourcebook on Child Sexual Abuse.* Newbury Park, CA: Sage Publications.

16. John Jay College of Criminal Justice. 2011. *The Causes and Context of Sexual Abuse of Minors by Catholic Priests in the United States, 1950–2010.* Washington, DC: United States Conference of Catholic Bishops, 13.

17. John Jay College of Criminal Justice. 2011. *The Causes and Context of Sexual Abuse of Minors by Catholic Priests in the United States, 1950–2010.* Washington, DC: United States Conference of Catholic Bishops), 4.

18. Doyle TP. 2007. Clericalism and Catholic Clergy Sexual Abuse. In: Frawley-O'Dea MG & Goldner V, editors. *Predatory Priests, Silenced Victims: the Sexual Abuse Crisis and the Catholic Church.* Mahwah, NJ: The Analytic Press; pp.147–162 at 159.

19. John Jay College of Criminal Justice. 2011. *The Causes and Context of Sexual Abuse of Minors by Catholic Priests in the United States, 1950–2010.* Washington, DC: United States Conference of Catholic Bishops, 3.

20. Pope John Paul II. 22 November 2001. Post-Synodal Apostolic Exhortation: *Ecclesia in Oceania.* The Vatican. Available from: <http://www.vatican.va/holy_father/john_paul_ii/apost_exhortations/documents/hf_jp-ii_exh_20011122_ecclesia-in-oceania_en.html> (accessed 24 January 2012).

Chapter 2

1. Radcliffe (O.P.) T. 2010. Come to Me All You Who Labour. In: Littleton J & Maher E, editors. *The Dublin/Murphy Report: a Watershed for Irish Catholicism?* Dublin: Columba Press; pp.17–28.

2. John Jay College of Criminal Justice. 2011. *The Causes and Context of Sexual Abuse of Minors by Catholic Priests in the United States, 1950–2010.* Washington, DC: United States Conference of Catholic Bishops.

3 Richter (1808–1864) AL, Gratian (12th C), Church of Rome & Pope Boniface VIII (1295–1303) et al. 2012. *Corpus Juris Canonici* (1879). University of Toronto Internet Archive. Available from: <http://www.archive.org/details/corpusjuriscanon00richuoft> (accessed 25 January 2012).

4 Doyle TP, Sipe AWR & Wall PJ. 2006. *Sex, Priests, and Secret Codes: the Catholic Church's 2000-Year Paper Trail of Sexual Abuse*. Los Angeles, CA: Volt Press.

5 The Editors. 7 June 1985. Priest Child Abuse Cases Victimizing Families; Bishops Lack Policy Response. National Catholic Reporter. Available from: <http://www.natcath.org/crisis/070585b.htm> (accessed 3 March 2012).

6 The General Counsel of the United States Conference of Catholic Bishops. 1988. USCCB Pedophilia Statement. *Origins* 17:624.

7 Winter GA, Commission of Enquiry into the Sexual Abuse of Children by Members of the Clergy & Archdiocese of St. John's. 1990. *The Report of the Archdiocesan Commission of Enquiry into the Sexual Abuse of Children by Members of the Clergy – Volume I*. St. John's, NL: Archdiocese of St. John's, 91.

8 Hogan L. 2011. Clerical and Religious Child Abuse: Ireland and Beyond. *Theological Studies* 72(1):170–186 at 172.

9 Canadian Conference of Catholic Bishops Ad Hoc Committee on Child Sexual Abuse & Canadian Conference of Catholic Bishops. 1992. *From Pain to Hope: Report From the CCCB Ad Hoc Committee on Child Sexual Abuse*. Ottawa, ON: Canadian Conference of Catholic Bishops.

10 Canadian Conference of Catholic Bishops Ad Hoc Committee on Child Sexual Abuse & Canadian Conference of Catholic Bishops. 1992. *Breach of Trust, Breach of Faith: Child Sexual Abuse in the Church and Society: Materials for Discussion Groups*. Ottawa, ON: Canadian Conference of Catholic Bishops.

11 United States Conference of Catholic Bishops. 1992. The Five Principles to Follow in Dealing with Accusations of Sexual Abuse. USCCB Office of Media Relations. Available from: <http://old.usccb.org/comm/kit4.shtml> (accessed 25 January 2012).

12 Pope John Paul II. 11 June 1993. Letter of His Holiness John Paul II to the Bishops of the United States of America, paragraph 2. The Vatican. Available from: <http://www.vatican.va/holy_father/john_paul_ii/letters/1993/documents/hf_jp-ii_let_19930611_vescovi-usa_en.html> (accessed 25 January 2012).

13 Lytton TD. 2008. *Holding Bishops Accountable: How Lawsuits Helped the Catholic Church Confront Clergy Sexual Abuse*. Cambridge, MA: Harvard University Press; Chinnici JP. 2010. *When Values Collide: the Catholic Church, Sexual Abuse, and the Challenges of Leadership*. Maryknoll, NY: Orbis Books; Lawler P. 2010. *The Faithful Departed: the Collapse of Boston's Catholic Culture*. New York, NY: Encounter Books.

14 Ioannes Paulus PP.II. 30 April 2001. *Litterae Apostolicae Motu Proprio Datae: Sacramentorum Sanctitatis Tutela. Quibus Normae De Gravioribus Delictis Congregationi Pro Docrtrina Fidei Reservatis Promulgantur*. The Vatican. Available from: <http://www.vatican.va/holy_father/john_paul_ii/motu_proprio/documents/hf_jp-ii_motu-proprio_20020110_sacramentorum-sanctitatis-tutela_lt.html> (accessed 3 March 2012); Pope John Paul II. 30 April 2001. *Sacramentorum Sanctitatis Tutela* (English Translation). BishopAccountability org. Available from: <http://www.bishop-accountability.org/resources/resource-files/churchdocs/SacramentorumAndNormaeEnglish.htm> (accessed 3 March 2012); Congregation for the Doctrine of the Faith. 21 May 2010. The Norms of the *Motu Proprio* "*Sacramentorum Sanctitatis Tutela*" (2001): Historical Introduction. The Vatican. Available from: <http://www.vatican.va/resources/resources_introd-storica_en.html> (accessed 3 March 2012).

15 The Investigative Staff of the Boston Globe. 2002. *Betrayal: the Crisis in the Catholic Church*. Boston, MA: Little, Brown and Company.

16 Lawler P. 2010. *The Faithful Departed: the Collapse of Boston's Catholic Culture*. New York, NY: Encounter Books.

17 United States Conference of Catholic Bishops. 2002. Charter for the Protection of Children and Young People. United States Conference of Catholic Bishops. Available from: <http://www.usccb.org/issues-and-action/child-and-youth-protection/charter.cfm> (accessed 25 January 2012).

18 John Jay College of Criminal Justice, Catholic Church & United States Conference of Catholic Bishops. 2004. *The Nature and Scope of Sexual Abuse of Minors by Catholic Priests and Deacons in the United States, 1950–2002*. Washington, DC: United States Conference of Catholic Bishops.

19 Pope Benedict XVI. 16 June 2009. Letter of His Holiness Pope Benedict XVI Proclaiming a Year for Priests on the 150th Anniversary of the "*Dies Natalis*" of the Curé of Ars. The Vatican. Available from: <http://www.vatican.va/holy_father/benedict_xvi/letters/2009/documents/hf_ben-xvi_let_20090616_anno-sacerdotale_en.html> (accessed 25 January 2012).

20 Pope Benedict XVI. 11 June 2010. Conclusion of the Year for Priests. Holy Mass. Homily of His Holiness Pope Benedict XVI. The Vatican. Available from: <http://www.vatican.va/holy_father/benedict_xvi/homilies/2010/documents/hf_ben-xvi_hom_20100611_concl-anno-sac_en.html> (accessed 25 January 2012).

21 John Jay College of Criminal Justice. 2011. *The Causes and Context of Sexual Abuse of Minors by Catholic Priests in the United States, 1950–2010*. Washington, DC: United States Conference of Catholic Bishops.

22 Justice Seán Ryan, Lowe F & Shanley M. 20 May 2009. Commission Report. The Commission to Inquire into Child Abuse (Ireland). Available from: <http://www.childabusecommission.com/rpt/> (accessed 25 January 2012).

23 Justice Yvonne Murphy, Mangan I & O'Neill H. 21 July 2009. Report by Commission of Investigation into Catholic Archdiocese of Dublin. Department of Justice and Equality (Ireland). Available from: <http://www.inis.gov.ie/en/JELR/Pages/PB09000504> (accessed 25 January 2012).

24 Lord Nolan, Swinton T, Abrahams C et al. 2001. A Programme for Action: Final Report of the Independent Review on Child Protection in the Catholic Church in England and Wales. Catholic Bishops' Conference of England and Wales. Available from: <http:\\www.bishop-accountability.org/resources/resource-files/reports/NolanReport.pdf> (accessed 25 January 2012).

25 Australian Bishops & Catholic Church. 1993. Pastoral Statement on Child Protection and Child Sexual Abuse (RCPS Exhibit 1803).

26 Deetman WJ, Draijer PJ, Kalbfleisch P et al. 16 December 2011. Commission of Inquiry into Sexual Abuse of Minors in the Roman Catholic Church. Onderzoekscommissie seksueel misbruik van minderjarigen binnen de Rooms Katholieke Kerk. Available from: <http://www.commissiedeetman.nl/english-summery.html> (accessed 25 January 2012).

27 Rigert J. 2008. *An Irish Tragedy: How Sex Abuse by Irish Priests Helped Cripple the Catholic Church*. Baltimore, MD: Crossland Press.

28 Murphy S. 2010. No Cheap Grace. *Studies: An Irish Quarterly Review* 99:303–316 at 307.

29 Allen Jr. JL. 7 February 2012. Vatican Abuse Summit: Expert Blasts Denial on Global Dimension of Crisis. National Catholic Reporter. Available from: <http://ncronline.org/blogs/ncr-today/vatican-abuse-summit-expert-blasts-denial-global-dimension-crisis> (accessed 3 March 2012).

30 Burke A, Bennett RS, Bland M et al. 27 February 2004. A Report on the Crisis in the Catholic Church in the United States, p. 94. Bishop-Accountability org. Available from: <http://www.bishop-accountability.org/usccb/causesandcontext/report-2004-02-27.htm> (accessed 25 January 2012).

31 Justice Yvonne Murphy, Mangan I & O'Neill H. 21 July 2009. Report by Commission of Investigation into Catholic Archdiocese of Dublin. Department of Justice and Equality (Ireland). Available from: <http://www.inis.gov.ie/en/JELR/Pages/PB09000504> (accessed 25 January 2012). 4,Pt.1.15

32 Curti E. 8 May 2010. Study in Scarlet: Clerical Sex-Abuse Scandal. The Tablet. Available from: <http://m.thetablet.co.uk/article/14665> (accessed 25 January 2012).

33 Winter GA, Commission of Enquiry into the Sexual Abuse of Children by Members of the Clergy & Archdiocese of St. John's, 1990, para 34. *The Report of the Archdiocesan Commission of Enquiry into the Sexual Abuse of Children by Members of the Clergy – Volume I*. St. John's, NL: Archdiocese of St. John's.

34 Canadian Conference of Catholic Bishops Ad Hoc Committee on Child Sexual Abuse & Canadian Conference of Catholic Bishops. 1992. *From Pain to Hope: Report from the CCCB Ad Hoc Committee on Child Sexual Abuse*. Ottawa, ON: Canadian Conference of Catholic Bishops.

35 United States Conference of Catholic Bishops. 1992. The Five Principles to Follow in Dealing with Accusations of Sexual Abuse. USCCB Office of Media Relations. Available from: <http://old.usccb.org/comm/kit4.shtml> (accessed 25 January 2012).

36 Robinson G. 2008. *Confronting Power and Sex in the Catholic Church: Reclaiming the Spirit of Jesus.* Collegeville, MN: Liturgical Press (originally published October 15, 2007, by Columba Press).

37 Archbishop Mark Coleridge. 23 May 2010. A Pentecost Letter on Sexual Abuse of the Young in the Catholic Church. The Archdiocese of Canberra Goulburn. Available from: <http://www.cg.catholic.org.au/about/default.cfm?loadref=359> (accessed 25 January 2012).

38 Irish Bishops. 9 December 2009. Statement from the Winter General Meeting of the Irish Bishops' Conference. Irish Catholic Bishops' Conference (ICBC general meetings, news archive 2009). Available from: <http://www.catholicbishops.ie/2009/12/09/statement-winter-general-meeting-irish-bishops-conference/> (accessed 25 January 2012).

39 Treacy B. 2010. Learning with Pope Benedict. *Doctrine and Life* 60(5. May–June):2–3 at 2.

40 Erlandson G & Bunson M. 2010. *Pope Benedict XVI and the Sexual Abuse Crisis: Working for Reform and Renewal.* Huntington, IN: Our Sunday Visitor Publishing Division.

41 Pope Benedict XVI. 20 December 2010. Address of His Holiness Benedict XVI on the Occasion of Christmas Greetings to the *Roman Curia*. The Vatican. Available from: <http://www.vatican.va/holy_father/benedict_xvi/speeches/2010/december/documents/hf_ben-xvi_spe_20101220_curia-auguri_en.html> (accessed 3 February 2012).

42 Pope Benedict XVI. 11 June 2010. Conclusion of the Year for Priests. Holy Mass. Homily of His Holiness Pope Benedict XVI. The Vatican. Available from: <http://www.vatican.va/holy_father/benedict_xvi/homilies/2010/documents/hf_ben-xvi_hom_20100611_concl-anno-sac_en.html> (accessed 25 January 2012).

43 Cardinal Tarcisio Bertone. 30 January 2012. Message of Cardinal Tarcisio Bertone on Behalf of His Holiness Pope Benedict XVI on the Occasion of the International Symposium "Towards Healing and Renewal". The Vatican. Available from: <http://www.vatican.va/roman_curia/secretariat_state/card-bertone/2012/documents/rc_seg-st_20120130_gregorian-university_en.html> (accessed 3 March 2012).

44 Pope John Paul II. 22 November 2001. Post-Synodal Apostolic Exhortation: *Ecclesia in Oceania*. The Vatican. Available from: <http://www.vatican.va/holy_father/john_paul_ii/apost_exhortations/documents/hf_jp-ii_exh_20011122_ecclesia-in-oceania_en.html> (accessed 24 January 2012).

Chapter 3

1 Pope Benedict XVI. 20 December 2010. Address of His Holiness Benedict XVI on the Occasion of Christmas Greetings to the *Roman Curia*. The Vatican. Available from: <http://www.vatican.va/holy_father/benedict_xvi/speeches/2010/december/documents/hf_ben-xvi_spe_20101220_curia-auguri_en.html> (accessed 3 February 2012).

2 Jenkins P. 2004. *Moral Panic: Changing Concepts of the Child Molester in Modern America.* New Haven, CT: Yale University Press.

3 Lytton TD. 2008. *Holding Bishops Accountable: How Lawsuits Helped the Catholic Church Confront Clergy Sexual Abuse.* Cambridge, MA: Harvard University Press; Chinnici JP. 2010. *When Values Collide: the Catholic Church, Sexual Abuse, and the Challenges of Leadership.* Maryknoll, NY: Orbis Books; Lawler P. 2010. *The Faithful Departed: the Collapse of Boston's Catholic Culture.* New York, NY: Encounter Books.

4 Weigel G. 2002. *The Courage to Be Catholic: Crisis, Reform and the Future of the Church.* New York, NY: Basic Books.

5 Pope S. 2006. Descriptions and Prescriptions: Proposed Remedies for a Church in Crisis. In: Cahill LS, Garvey J & Kennedy TF, editors. *Sexuality and the U.S. Catholic Church: Crisis and Renewal.* New York, NY: Herder & Herder Book/Crossroad Publishing Company; pp.183–195.

6. Clifford AM. 2001. *Introducing Feminist Theology*. Maryknoll, NY: Orbis Books.

7. Cahill LS. 2004. Feminist Theology and a Participatory Church. In: Pope SJ, editor. *Common Calling: the Laity and Governance of the Catholic Church*. Washington, DC: Georgetown University Press; pp.117–150.

8. Ammicht-Quinn R, Haker H & Junker-Kenny M. 2004. *The Structural Betrayal of Trust*. 3rd ed. London: SCM Press.

9. O'Meara NM. 2006. Rebuilding Community: Credibility, Sensitivity and Hope. In: Cahill LS, Garvey J & Kennedy TF, editors. *Sexuality and the U.S. Catholic Church: Crisis and Renewal*. New York: Herder & Herder Book/Crossroad Publishing Company; pp.7–17 at 8.

10. National Federation for Catholic Youth Ministry. 4 February 2012. NFCYM website. Available from: <http://www.nfcym.org/> (accessed 4 February 2012).

11. Doyle TP, Sipe AWR & Wall PJ. 2006. *Sex, Priests, and Secret Codes: the Catholic Church's 2000-Year Paper Trail of Sexual Abuse*. Los Angeles, CA: Volt Press; Wilson GB. 2008. *Clericalism: the Death of the Priesthood*. Collegeville, MN: The Liturgical Press; Papesh ML. 2004. *Clerical Culture: Contradiction and Transformation – the Culture of the Diocesan Priests of the United States Catholic Church*. Collegeville, MN: Liturgical Press.

12. Pope Benedict XVI. 16 June 2009. Letter of His Holiness Pope Benedict XVI Proclaiming a Year for Priests on the 150th Anniversary of the "*Dies Natalis*" of the Curé of Ars. The Vatican. Available from: <http://www.vatican.va/holy_father/benedict_xvi/letters/2009/documents/hf_ben-xvi_let_20090616_anno-sacerdotale_en.html> (accessed 25 January 2012).

13. Catanzaro AM. 17 June 2011. The Fog of Scandal: the Chair of the Philadelphia Review Board Speaks. Commonweal. Available from: <http://commonwealmagazine.org/fog-scandal-1> (accessed 4 February 2012).

14. Schuth K. 1999. *Seminaries, Theologates, and the Future of Church Ministry: an Analysis of Trends and Transitions*. Collegeville, MN: Liturgical Press.

15. John Jay College of Criminal Justice. 2011. *The Causes and Context of Sexual Abuse of Minors by Catholic Priests in the United States, 1950–2010*. Washington, DC: United States Conference of Catholic Bishops.

16. Pope John Paul II. 12 March 1992. Post-Synodal Apostolic Exhortation: *Pastores Dabo Vobis*. The Vatican. Available from: <http://www.vatican.va/holy_father/john_paul_ii/apost_exhortations/documents/hf_jp-ii_exh_25031992_pastores-dabo-vobis_en.html> (accessed 4 February 2012).

17. United States Conference of Catholic Bishops. 2006. Program of Priestly Formation (5th Edition). USCCB website. Available from: <http://old.usccb.org/vocations/ProgramforPriestlyFormation.pdf> (accessed 2 April 2012).

18. Schuth K. 2011. Assessing the Education of Priests and Lay Ministries: Content and Consequences. In: Lacey MJ & Oakley F, editors. *The Crisis of Authority in Catholic Modernity*. New York, NY: Oxford University Press; pp.317–348 at 339.

19. Canadian Conference of Catholic Bishops Ad Hoc Committee on Child Sexual Abuse & Canadian Conference of Catholic Bishops. 1992. *From Pain to Hope: Report From the CCCB Ad Hoc Committee on Child Sexual Abuse*. Ottawa, ON: Canadian Conference of Catholic Bishops.

20. United States Conference of Catholic Bishops. 1992. The Five Principles to Follow in Dealing with Accusations of Sexual Abuse. USCCB Office of Media Relations. Available from: <http://old.usccb.org/comm/kit4.shtml> (accessed 25 January 2012).

21. United States Conference of Catholic Bishops. 2002. Charter for the Protection of Children and Young People. United States Conference of Catholic Bishops. Available from: <http://www.usccb.org/issues-and-action/child-and-youth-protection/charter.cfm> (accessed 25 January 2012).

22. VIRTUS Online. 2012. A program and service of The National Catholic Risk Retention Group, Inc. Available from: <http://www.virtus.org/virtus/> (accessed 4 February 2012).

23 Cardinal William Levada. 6 February 2012. The Sexual Abuse of Minors: a Multi-Faceted Response to the Challenge. Zenit org. Available from: <http://www.zenit.org/article-34242?l=english> (accessed 3 March 2012).

24 Cardinal Marc Ouellet. 7 February 2012. Homily for the Penitential Vigil on the Occasion of the Symposium "Towards Healing and Renewal". Canadian Conference of Catholic Bishops. Available from: <http://www.cccb.ca/site/images/stories/pdf/Cardinal_Ouellet_Prayer_Service_Rome_2012.pdf> (accessed 3 March 2012).

25 Allen Jr. JL. 6 January 2012. O'Malley on the Sex Abuse Crisis: 'It's Not Behind Us'. National Catholic Reporter. Available from: <http://ncronline.org/blogs/all-things-catholic/omalley-sex-abuse-crisis-its-not-behind-us> (accessed 4 February 2012).

26 Pope Benedict XVI. 20 December 2010. Address of His Holiness Benedict XVI on the Occasion of Christmas Greetings to the *Roman Curia*. The Vatican. Available from: <http://www.vatican.va/holy_father/benedict_xvi/speeches/2010/december/documents/hf_ben-xvi_spe_20101220_curia-auguri_en.html> (accessed 3 February 2012).

27 Archbishop Mark Coleridge. 23 May 2010. A Pentecost Letter on Sexual Abuse of the Young in the Catholic Church. The Archdiocese of Canberra Goulburn. Available from: <http://www.cg.catholic.org.au/about/default.cfm?loadref=359> (accessed 25 January 2012).

28 Littleton J & Maher E. 2010. *The Dublin/Murphy Report: A Watershed for Irish Catholicism?* Dublin: Columba Press. Italics added.

29 Archbishop Anthony Mancini. 2 October 2009. Letter to the Roman Catholic Faithful of Nova Scotia. Archdiocese of Halifax. Available from: <www.catholichalifax.org/images/stories/BishopOffice/2009 10 02 All RC of NS.pdf > (accessed 24 January 2012).

30 Hogan L. 2011. Clerical and Religious Child Abuse: Ireland and Beyond. *Theological Studies* 72(1):170–186 at 179.

31 Pope Benedict XVI. 19 March 2010. Pastoral Letter of the Holy Father Pope Benedict XVI to the Catholics of Ireland. The Vatican. Available from: <http://www.vatican.va/holy_father/benedict_xvi/letters/2010/documents/hf_ben-xvi_let_20100319_church-ireland_en.html> (accessed 24 January 2012).

32 Pope John Paul II. 22 November 2001. Post-Synodal Apostolic Exhortation: *Ecclesia in Oceania*. The Vatican. Available from: <http://www.vatican.va/holy_father/john_paul_ii/apost_exhortations/documents/hf_jp-ii_exh_20011122_ecclesia-in-oceania_en.html> (accessed 24 January 2012).

Chapter 4

1 Pope Paul VI. 21 November 1964. Dogmatic Constitutions on the Church: *Lumen Gentium*. The Vatican. Available from: <http://www.vatican.va/archive/hist_councils/ii_vatican_council/documents/vat-ii_const_19641121_lumen-gentium_en.html> (accessed 24 January 2012).

2 Papesh ML. 2004. *Clerical Culture: Contradiction and Transformation – the Culture of the Diocesan Priests of the United States Catholic Church.* Collegeville, MN: Liturgical Press.

3 Wilson GB. 2008. *Clericalism: the Death of the Priesthood.* Collegeville, MN: The Liturgical Press.

4 Papesh ML. 2004. *Clerical Culture: Contradiction and Transformation – the Culture of the Diocesan Priests of the United States Catholic Church*. Collegeville, MN: Liturgical Press, 17.

5 Hoge DR. 2002. *The First Five Years of Priesthood: a Study of Newly Ordained Catholic Priests*. Collegeville, MN: Liturgical Press; Hoge DR & Wenger JE. 2003. *Evolving Visions of the Priesthood: Changes from Vatican II to the Turn of the Century*. Collegeville, MN: Liturgical Press.

6 Papesh ML. 2004. *Clerical Culture: Contradiction and Transformation – the Culture of the Diocesan Priests of the United States Catholic Church*. Collegeville, MN: Liturgical Press, 21.

7 O'Meara TF. 1999. *Theology of Ministry*. Rev. ed. New York, NY: Paulist Press, 102.

8 Doyle T. 2006. Clericalism: Enabler of Clergy Sexual Abuse. *Pastoral Psychology* 54(3):189–213 at 194.

9. Papesh ML. 2004. *Clerical Culture: Contradiction and Transformation – the Culture of the Diocesan Priests of the United States Catholic Church.* Collegeville, MN: Liturgical Press, 36.

10. O'Meara TF. 1999. *Theology of Ministry.* Rev. ed. New York, NY: Paulist Press; Bernier P. 1992. *Ministry in the Church: a Historical and Pastoral Approach.* Mystic, CT: Twenty-Third Publications.

11. Lakeland P. 2004. *The Liberation of the Laity: in Search of an Accountable Church.* New York, NY: The Continuum International Publishing Group.

12. Pope Benedict XVI. 16 June 2009. Letter of His Holiness Pope Benedict XVI Proclaiming a Year for Priests on the 150th Anniversary of the "*Dies Natalis*" of the Curé of Ars. The Vatican. Available from: <http://www.vatican.va/holy_father/benedict_xvi/letters/2009/documents/hf_ben-xvi_let_20090616_anno-sacerdotale_en.html> (accessed 25 January 2012).

13. O'Malley JW. 2008. *What Happened at Vatican II.* Cambridge, MA: Belknap Press of Harvard University Press.

14. Gallagher MP. 2003. *Clashing Cymbals: an Introduction to Faith and Culture.* New York, NY: Paulist Press.

15. Doyle TP. 2007. Clericalism and Catholic Clergy Sexual Abuse. In: Frawley-O'Dea MG & Goldner V, editors. *Predatory Priests, Silenced Victims: the Sexual Abuse Crisis and the Catholic Church.* Mahwah, NJ: The Analytic Press; pp.147–162 at 147.

16. Conference of Major Superiors of Men. 2007. In Solidarity and Service: Reflections on the Problem of Clericalism in the Church. In: Frawley-O'Dea MG, editor. *Perversion of Power: Sexual Abuse in the Catholic Church.* 1st ed. Nashville, TN: Vanderbilt University Press. qtd. on 151.

17. Wilson GB. 2008. *Clericalism: the Death of the Priesthood.* Collegeville, MN: The Liturgical Press.

18. Cozzens DB. 2002. *Sacred Silence: Denial and the Crisis in the Church.* Collegeville, MN: Liturgical Press.

19. Papesh ML. 2004. *Clerical Culture: Contradiction and Transformation – the Culture of the Diocesan Priests of the United States Catholic Church.* Collegeville, MN: Liturgical Press.

20. Doyle TP. 2007. Clericalism and Catholic Clergy Sexual Abuse. In: Frawley-O'Dea MG & Goldner V, editors. *Predatory Priests, Silenced Victims: the Sexual Abuse Crisis and the Catholic Church.* Mahwah, NJ: The Analytic Press; pp.147–162 at 158.

21. Radcliffe (O.P.) T. 2010. Come to Me All You Who Labour. In: Littleton J & Maher E, editors. *The Dublin/Murphy Report: a Watershed for Irish Catholicism?* Dublin: Columba Press; pp.17–28 at 24–25.

22. John Jay College of Criminal Justice. 2011. *The Causes and Context of Sexual Abuse of Minors by Catholic Priests in the United States, 1950–2010.* Washington, DC: United States Conference of Catholic Bishops.

23. Steinfels P. 2003. *A People Adrift: the Crisis of the Roman Catholic Church in America.* New York, NY: Simon & Schuster.

24. Doyle TP, Sipe AWR & Wall PJ. 2006. *Sex, Priests, and Secret Codes: the Catholic Church's 2000-Year Paper Trail of Sexual Abuse.* Los Angeles, CA: Volt Press.

25. Pope John Paul II. 22 November 2001. Post-Synodal Apostolic Exhortation: *Ecclesia in Oceania.* The Vatican. Available from: <http://www.vatican.va/holy_father/john_paul_ii/apost_exhortations/documents/hf_jp-ii_exh_20011122_ecclesia-in-oceania_en.html> (accessed 24 January 2012).

Chapter 5

1. Rolheiser R. 1999. *The Holy Longing: The Search for a Christian Spirituality.* 1st in the U.S.A. ed. New York, NY: Doubleday, 96.

2. O'Hanlon G. 2010. The Murphy Report: a Response. *The Furrow* 61:82–91.

3. Doyle TP, Sipe AWR & Wall PJ. 2006. *Sex, Priests, and Secret Codes: the Catholic Church's 2000-Year Paper Trail of Sexual Abuse.* Los Angeles, CA: Volt Press.

4 Ammicht-Quinn R, Haker H & Junker-Kenny M. 2004. *The Structural Betrayal of Trust*. 3rd ed. London: SCM Press.

5 Traina C. 2003. Sex in the *City of God. Currents in Theology and Mission* 30:5–19.

6 O'Malley JW. 2008. *What Happened at Vatican II*. Cambridge, MA: Belknap Press of Harvard University Press.

7 Rigali N. 1998. On the *Humanae Vitae* Process: Ethics of Teaching Morality. *Louvain Studies* 2:3–21.

8 Pope Paul VI. 25 July 1968. Encyclical Letter *Humanae Vitae*. The Vatican. Available from: <http://www.vatican.va/holy_father/paul_vi/encyclicals/documents/hf_p-vi_enc_25071968_humanae-vitae_en.html> (accessed 12 February 2012).

9 Cahill LS, Garvey J & Kennedy TF. 2006. *Sexuality and the U.S. Catholic Church: Crisis and Renewal*. New York: Herder & Herder Book/Crossroad Publishing Company; Keenan J. 2005. Notes on Moral Theology: Ethics and the Crisis in the Church. *Theological Studies* 66:117–136.

10 McCormick R. 1999. Moral Theology 1940–1989: an Overview. In: Curran CE & McCormick RA, editors. *The Historical Development of Fundamental Moral Theology in the United States*. New York, NY: Paulist Press; pp.46–74.

11 Häring B. 1978. *Free and Faithful in Christ: Moral Theology for Clergy and Laity*. New York: Seabury Press, 12.

12 Häring B & Kaiser (trans.) E. 1967. *The Law of Christ: Moral Theology for Priests and Laity, Vols. I–III*. Westminster, MD: Newman Press, vii.

13 Pope John Paul II. 1997. *The Theology of the Body: Human Love in the Divine Plan*. Boston, MA: Pauline Books & Media.

14 West C. 2003. *Theology of the Body Explained: a Commentary on John Paul II's "Gospel of the Body"*. Boston, MA: Pauline Books & Media.

15 Cloutier D. 2006. "Heaven Is a Place on Earth?" Analyzing the Popularity of Pope John Paul II's Theology of the Body. In: Cahill LS, Garvey J & Kennedy TF, editors. *Sexuality and the U.S. Catholic Church: Crisis and Renewal*. New York, NY: Herder & Herder Book/Crossroad Publishing Company; pp.18–31.

16 Johnson LT. 2001. A Disembodied "Theology of the Body": John Paul II on Love, Sex & Pleasure. *Commonweal* 128(2):11–17.

17 Johnson, p. 13.

18 Salzman TA. 2008. *The Sexual Person: Toward a Renewed Catholic Anthropology*. Washington, DC: Georgetown University Press.

19 Rolheiser R. 1999. *The Holy Longing: The Search for a Christian Spirituality*. 1st in the U.S.A. ed. New York, NY: Doubleday, 192–193.

20 Keenan JF. 2010. *A History of Catholic Moral Theology in the Twentieth Century: From Confessing Sins to Liberating Consciences*. London: Continuum International Publishing Group.

21 Rigali N. 2007. Moral Theology and Church Responses to Sexual Abuse. *Horizons* 34(2):183–204.

22 Pope John Paul II. 22 November 2001. Post-Synodal Apostolic Exhortation: *Ecclesia in Oceania*. The Vatican. Available from: <http://www.vatican.va/holy_father/john_paul_ii/apost_exhortations/documents/hf_jp-ii_exh_20011122_ecclesia-in-oceania_en.html> (accessed 24 January 2012).

Chapter 6

1 Cardinal Tarcisio Bertone. 30 January 2012. Message of Cardinal Tarcisio Bertone on Behalf of His Holiness Pope Benedict XVI on the Occasion of the International Symposium "Towards Healing and Renewal". The Vatican. Available from: <http://www.vatican.va/roman_curia/secretariat_state/card-bertone/2012/documents/rc_seg-st_20120130_gregorian-university_en.html> (accessed 3 March 2012).

2   Dulles AR. 1987. *Models of the Church*. Expanded ed. Garden City, NY: Image Books.

3   Pope John Paul II. 22 November 2001. Post-Synodal Apostolic Exhortation: *Ecclesia in Oceania*. The Vatican. Available from: <http://www.vatican.va/holy_father/john_paul_ii/apost_exhortations/documents/hf_jp-ii_exh_20011122_ecclesia-in-oceania_en.html> (accessed 24 January 2012).

4   Eterovic N & The General Secretariat of the Synod of Bishops and Libreria Editrice Vaticana. 2 February 2011. Synod of Bishops, XIII Ordinary General Assembly: The New Evangelization for the Transmission of the Christian Church. *Lineamenta*, section 5. The Vatican. Available from: <http://www.vatican.va/roman_curia/synod/documents/rc_synod_doc_20110202_lineamenta-xiii-assembly_en.html> (accessed 3 March 2012).

5   Frawley-O'Dea MG. 2007. *Perversion of Power: Sexual Abuse in the Catholic Church*. 1st ed. Nashville, TN: Vanderbilt University Press, 5:9 & 151–157.

6   Wilson GB. 2008. *Clericalism: the Death of the Priesthood*. Collegeville, MN: The Liturgical Press.

7   Conway E. 2004. Operative Theologies of Priesthood: Have They Contributed to Child Sexual Abuse? In: Ammicht-Quinn R, Haker H & Junker-Kenny M, editors. *The Structural Betrayal of Trust*. London: SCM Press; pp.72–86.

8   Pope John Paul II. 22 November 2001. Post-Synodal Apostolic Exhortation: *Ecclesia in Oceania*. The Vatican. Available from: <http://www.vatican.va/holy_father/john_paul_ii/apost_exhortations/documents/hf_jp-ii_exh_20011122_ecclesia-in-oceania_en.html> (accessed 24 January 2012).

9   Pope Paul VI. 21 November 1964. Dogmatic Constitutions on the Church: *Lumen Gentium*, no. 39 and 40. The Vatican. Available from: <http://www.vatican.va/archive/hist_councils/ii_vatican_council/documents/vat-ii_const_19641121_lumen-gentium_en.html> (accessed 24 January 2012).

10 *Lumen Gentium*, no. 10.

11 Wilson GB. 2008. *Clericalism: the Death of the Priesthood*. Collegeville, MN: The Liturgical Press, 42–43.

12 *Lumen Gentium*, 32.

13 Pope John Paul II. 30 December 1988. Post-Synodal Apostolic Exhortation: *Christifideles Laici*. The Vatican. Available from: <http://www.vatican.va/holy_father/john_paul_ii/apost_exhortations/documents/hf_jp-ii_exh_30121988_christifideles-laici_en.html> (accessed 3 March 2012).

14 See also *Lumen Gentium*, no. 10.

15 Pope John Paul II. 16 October 2003. Post-Synodal Apostolic Exhortation: *Pastores Gregis*, no. 44. The Vatican. Available from: <http://www.vatican.va/holy_father/john_paul_ii/apost_exhortations/documents/hf_jp-ii_exh_20031016_pastores-gregis_en.html> (accessed 3 March 2012).

16 Häring B & Kaiser (trans.) E. 1967. *The Law of Christ: Moral Theology for Priests and Laity, Vols. I–III*. Westminster, MD: Newman Press, vii.

17 Cardinal Tarcisio Bertone. 30 January 2012. Message of Cardinal Tarcisio Bertone on Behalf of His Holiness Pope Benedict XVI on the Occasion of the International Symposium "Towards Healing and Renewal". The Vatican. Available from: <http://www.vatican.va/roman_curia/secretariat_state/card-bertone/2012/documents/rc_seg-st_20120130_gregorian-university_en.html> (accessed 3 March 2012).

18 Pope John Paul II. 22 November 2001. Post-Synodal Apostolic Exhortation: *Ecclesia in Oceania*. The Vatican. Available from: <http://www.vatican.va/holy_father/john_paul_ii/apost_exhortations/documents/hf_jp-ii_exh_20011122_ecclesia-in-oceania_en.html> (accessed 24 January 2012).

19 Archbishop Diarmuid Martin. 20 March 2010. Homily Fifth Sunday of Lent (Papal Letter). Archdiocese of Dublin. Available from: <http://www.dublindiocese.ie/content/2032010-homily-fifth-sunday-lent-papal-letter> (accessed 3 March 2012).

20 Brueggemann W. 2001. *The Prophetic Imagination*. 2nd ed. Minneapolis, MN: Augsburg Fortress.

21 The Holy Roman Catholic Church. 2012. *Catechism of the Catholic Church*, no. 1817. The Vatican. Available from: <http://www.vatican.va/archive/ccc_css/archive/catechism/ccc_toc.htm> (accessed 3 March 2012).

BIBLIOGRAPHY

The Holy Bible: New Revised Standard Version. 1989. New York, NY: Oxford University Press.

Allen Jr. JL. 6 January 2012. O'Malley on the Sex Abuse Crisis: 'It's Not Behind Us'. National Catholic Reporter. Available from: <http://ncronline.org/blogs/all-things-catholic/omalley-sex-abuse-crisis-its-not-behind-us> (accessed 4 February 2012).

Allen Jr. JL. 7 February 2012. Vatican Abuse Summit: Expert Blasts Denial on Global Dimension of Crisis. National Catholic Reporter. Available from: <http://ncronline.org/blogs/ncr-today/vatican-abuse-summit-expert-blasts-denial-global-dimension-crisis> (accessed 3 March 2012).

Ammicht-Quinn R, Haker H & Junker-Kenny M. 2004. *The Structural Betrayal of Trust.* 3rd ed. London: SCM Press.

Archbishop Anthony Mancini. 2 October 2009. Letter to the Roman Catholic Faithful of Nova Scotia. Archdiocese of Halifax. Available from: <www.catholichalifax.org/images/stories/BishopOffice/2009 10 02 All RC of NS.pdf > (accessed 24 January 2012).

Archbishop Diarmuid Martin. 20 March 2010. Homily Fifth Sunday of Lent (Papal Letter). Archdiocese of Dublin. Available from: <http://www.dublindiocese.ie/content/2032010-homily-fifth-sunday-lent-papal-letter> (accessed 3 March 2012).

Archbishop Mark Coleridge. 23 May 2010. A Pentecost Letter on Sexual Abuse of the Young in the Catholic Church. The Archdiocese of Canberra Goulburn. Available from: <http://www.cg.catholic.org.au/about/default.cfm?loadref=359> (accessed 25 January 2012).

Australian Bishops & Catholic Church. 1993. Pastoral Statement on Child Protection and Child Sexual Abuse (RCPS Exhibit 1803).

Bergeron G. 2004. *Don't Call Me a Victim*. Lowell, MA: King Printing Company.

Bernier P. 1992. *Ministry in the Church: a Historical and Pastoral Approach*. Mystic, CT: Twenty-Third Publications.

Bernier R, Cere D, Kenny N, Padamadan S & Waind J. 2012. Trauma and Transformation: the Catholic Church and the Sexual Abuse Crisis. Conference Website and Posted Proceedings, McGill University, 14-15 October 2011. McGill University Centre for Research on Religion. Available from: <http://traumaandtransformation.org/> (accessed 24 January 2012).

Berry J. 2000. *Lead Us Not into Temptation: Catholic Priests and the Sexual Abuse of Children*. 1st Illinois paperback ed. Urbana, IL: University of Illinois Press.

Brueggemann W. 2001. *The Prophetic Imagination*. 2nd ed. Minneapolis, MN: Augsburg Fortress.

Burke A, Bennett RS, Bland M et al. 27 February 2004. A Report on the Crisis in the Catholic Church in the United States. Bishop-Accountability org. Available from: <http://www.bishop-accountability.org/usccb/causesandcontext/report-2004-02-27.htm> (accessed 25 January 2012).

Cahill LS. 2004. Feminist Theology and a Participatory Church. In: Pope SJ, editor. *Common Calling: the Laity and Governance of the Catholic Church*. Washington, DC: Georgetown University Press; pp.117–150.

Cahill LS, Garvey J & Kennedy TF. 2006. *Sexuality and the U.S. Catholic Church: Crisis and Renewal*. New York: Herder & Herder Book/Crossroad Publishing Company.

Canadian Council of Catholic Bishops Ad Hoc Committee on Child Sexual Abuse & Canadian Conference of Catholic Bishops. 1992. *Breach of Trust, Breach of Faith: Child Sexual Abuse in the Church and Society: Materials for Discussion Groups*. Ottawa, ON: Canadian Conference of Catholic Bishops.

Canadian Council of Catholic Bishops Ad Hoc Committee on Child Sexual Abuse & Canadian Conference of Catholic Bishops. 1992. *From Pain to Hope: Report from the CCCB Ad Hoc Committee on Child Sexual Abuse*. Ottawa, ON: Canadian Conference of Catholic Bishops.

Cardinal Marc Ouellet. 7 February 2012. Homily for the Penitential Vigil on the Occasion of the Symposium "Towards Healing and Renewal". Canadian Conference of Catholic Bishops. Available from: <http://www.cccb.ca/site/images/stories/pdf/Cardinal_Ouellet_Prayer_Service_Rome_2012.pdf> (accessed 3 March 2012).

Cardinal Tarcisio Bertone. 30 January 2012. Message of Cardinal Tarcisio Bertone on Behalf of His Holiness Pope Benedict XVI on the Occasion of the International Symposium "Towards Healing and Renewal". The Vatican. Available from: <http://www.vatican.va/roman_curia/secretariat_state/card-bertone/2012/documents/rc_seg-st_20120130_gregorian-university_en.html> (accessed 3 March 2012).

Cardinal William Levada. 6 February 2012. The Sexual Abuse of Minors: a Multi-Faceted Response to the Challenge. Zenit org. Available from: <http://www.zenit.org/article-34242?l=english> (accessed 3 March 2012).

Catanzaro AM. 17 June 2011. The Fog of Scandal: the Chair of the Philadelphia Review Board Speaks. Commonweal. Available from: <http://commonwealmagazine.org/fog-scandal-1> (accessed 4 February 2012).

Catherine of Siena & Noffke S. 2000. *The Letters of Catherine of Siena*. Rev. ed. Tempe, AZ: Arizona Center for Medieval and Renaissance Studies.

Cere D. May 2010. Toward a Gospel Witness: Confronting Child Abuse. Homiletic and Pastoral Review. Available from: <http://www.catholiceducation.org/articles/apologetics/ap0344.htm> (accessed 11 May 2011).

Chinnici JP. 2010. *When Values Collide: the Catholic Church, Sexual Abuse, and the Challenges of Leadership*. Maryknoll, NY: Orbis Books.

Clifford AM. 2001. *Introducing Feminist Theology*. Maryknoll, NY: Orbis Books.

Cloutier D. 2006. "Heaven Is a Place on Earth?" Analyzing the Popularity of Pope John Paul II's Theology of the Body. In: Cahill LS, Garvey J & Kennedy TF, editors. *Sexuality and the U.S. Catholic Church: Crisis and Renewal*. New York, NY: Herder & Herder Book/Crossroad Publishing Company; pp.18–31.

Conference of Major Superiors of Men. 2007. In Solidarity and Service: Reflections on the Problem of Clericalism in the Church. In: Frawley-O'Dea MG, editor. *Perversion of Power: Sexual Abuse in the Catholic Church*. 1st ed. Nashville, TN: Vanderbilt University Press.

Congregation for the Doctrine of the Faith. 21 May 2010. The Norms of the *Motu Proprio "Sacramentorum Sanctitatis Tutela"* (2001): Historical Introduction. The Vatican. Available from: <http://www.vatican.va/resources/resources_introd-storica_en.html> (accessed 3 March 2012).

Conway E. 2004. Operative Theologies of Priesthood: Have They Contributed to Child Sexual Abuse? In: Ammicht-Quinn R, Haker H & Junker-Kenny M, editors. *The Structural Betrayal of Trust*. London: SCM Press; pp. 72–86.

Cozzens DB. 2002. *Sacred Silence: Denial and the Crisis in the Church*. Collegeville, MN: Liturgical Press.

Curti E. 8 May 2010. Study in Scarlet: Clerical Sex-Abuse Scandal. The Tablet. Available from: <http://m.thetablet.co.uk/article/14665> (accessed 25 January 2012).

DeCosse D. 2007. Freedom of the Press and Catholic Social Thought. *Theological Studies* 68:865–899.

Deetman WJ, Draijer PJ, Kalbfleisch P et al. 16 December 2011. Commission of Inquiry into Sexual Abuse of Minors in the Roman Catholic Church. Onderzoekscommissie seksueel misbruik van minderjarigen binnen de Rooms Katholieke Kerk. Available from: <http://www.commissiedeetman.nl/english-summery.html> (accessed 25 January 2012).

Doyle T. 2006. Clericalism: Enabler of Clergy Sexual Abuse. *Pastoral Psychology* 54(3):189–213.

Doyle TP. 2007. Clericalism and Catholic Clergy Sexual Abuse. In: Frawley-O'Dea MG & Goldner V, editors. *Predatory Priests, Silenced Victims: the Sexual Abuse Crisis and the Catholic Church*. Mahwah, NJ: The Analytic Press; pp.147–162.

Doyle TP, Sipe AWR & Wall PJ. 2006. *Sex, Priests, and Secret Codes: the Catholic Church's 2000-Year Paper Trail of Sexual Abuse*. Los Angeles, CA: Volt Press.

Dulles AR. 1987. *Models of the Church*. Expanded ed. Garden City, NY: Image Books.

Erlandson G & Bunson M. 2010. *Pope Benedict XVI and the Sexual Abuse Crisis: Working for Reform and Renewal*. Huntington, IN: Our Sunday Visitor Publishing Division.

Estrada H. 2011. *UnHoly Communion: Lessons Learned from Life Among Pedophiles, Predators, and Priests*. New Mexico: Red Rabbit Press.

Eterovic N & The General Secretariat of the Synod of Bishops and Libreria Editrice Vaticana. 2 February 2011. Synod of Bishops, XIII Ordinary General Assembly: The New Evangelization for the Transmission of the Christian Church. *Lineamenta*. The Vatican. Available from: <http://www.vatican.va/roman_curia/synod/documents/rc_synod_doc_20110202_lineamenta-xiii-assembly_en.html> (accessed 3 March 2012).

Finkelhor D & Araji S. 1986. *A Sourcebook on Child Sexual Abuse*. Newbury Park, CA: Sage Publications.

Finkelhor D & Jones LM. January 2004. Explanations for the Decline in Child Sexual Abuse Cases. United States Department of Justice, Office of Justice Programs, Office of Juvenile Justice and Delinquency Prevention. Available from: <http://purl.access.gpo.gov/GPO/LPS44917>

Fortune MM. 1999. *Is Nothing Sacred? The Story of a Pastor, the Women He Sexually Abused, and the Congregation He Nearly Destroyed*. Cleveland, OH: United Church Press.

Frawley-O'Dea MG. 2007. *Perversion of Power: Sexual Abuse in the Catholic Church*. 1st ed. Nashville, TN: Vanderbilt University Press.

Frawley-O'Dea MG & Goldner V. 2007. *Predatory Priests, Silenced Victims: the Sexual Abuse Crisis and the Catholic Church*. Mahwah, NJ: The Analytic Press.

Galasso C. 2007. *Crosses: Portraits of Clergy Abuse*. London: Trolley Ltd.

Gallagher MP. 2003. *Clashing Cymbals: an Introduction to Faith and Culture*. New York, NY: Paulist Press.

Häring B. 1978. *Free and Faithful in Christ: Moral Theology for Clergy and Laity*. New York: Seabury Press.

Häring B & Kaiser (trans.) E. 1967. *The Law of Christ: Moral Theology for Priests and Laity, Vols. I - III*. Westminster, MD: Newman Press.

Heschel AJ & Heschel S. 2001. *Moral Grandeur and Spiritual Audacity Essays*. 4th pbk. ed. New York, NY: Farrar, Straus & Giroux.

Higgins MW & Kavanagh P. 2010. *Suffer the Children Unto Me: an Open Inquiry into the Clerical Sex Abuse Scandal*. Toronto: Novalis.

Hogan L. 2011. Clerical and Religious Child Abuse: Ireland and Beyond. *Theological Studies* 72(1):170–186.

Hoge DR. 2002. *The First Five Years of Priesthood: a Study of Newly Ordained Catholic Priests*. Collegeville, MN: Liturgical Press.

Hoge DR & Wenger JE. 2003. *Evolving Visions of the Priesthood: Changes from Vatican II to the Turn of the Century*. Collegeville, MN: Liturgical Press.

Ioannes Paulus PP.II. 30 April 2001. *Litterae Apostolicae Motu Proprio Datae: Sacramentorum Sanctitatis Tutela. Quibus Normae De Gravioribus Delictis Congregationi Pro Docrtrina Fidei Reservatis Promulgantur*. The Vatican. Available from: <http://www.vatican.va/holy_father/john_paul_ii/motu_proprio/documents/hf_jp-ii_motu-proprio_20020110_sacramentorum-sanctitatis-tutela_lt.html> (accessed 3 March 2012).

Irish Bishops. 9 December 2009. Statement from the Winter General Meeting of the Irish Bishops' Conference. Irish Catholic Bishops' Conference (ICBC general meetings, news archive 2009). Available from: <http://www.catholicbishops.ie/2009/12/09/statement-winter-general-meeting-irish-bishops-conference/> (accessed 25 January 2012).

Jenkins P. 2004. *Moral Panic: Changing Concepts of the Child Molester in Modern America*. New Haven, CT: Yale University Press.

John Jay College of Criminal Justice. 2011. *The Causes and Context of Sexual Abuse of Minors by Catholic Priests in the United States, 1950–2010*. Washington, DC: United States Conference of Catholic Bishops.

John Jay College of Criminal Justice, Catholic Church & United States Conference of Catholic Bishops. 2004. *The Nature and Scope of Sexual Abuse of Minors by Catholic Priests and Deacons in the United States, 1950–2002*. Washington, DC: United States Conference of Catholic Bishops.

Johnson LT. 2001. A Disembodied "Theology of the Body": John Paul II on Love, Sex & Pleasure. *Commonweal* 128(2):11–17.

Justice Seán Ryan, Lowe F & Shanley M. 20 May 2009. Commission Report. The Commission to Inquire into Child Abuse (Ireland). Available from: <http://www.childabusecommission.com/rpt/> (accessed 25 January 2012).

Justice Yvonne Murphy, Mangan I & O'Neill H. 21 July 2009. Report by Commission of Investigation into Catholic Archdiocese of Dublin. Department of Justice and Equality (Ireland). Available from: <http://www.inis.gov.ie/en/JELR/Pages/PB09000504> (accessed 03 April 2012).

Keenan J. 2005. Notes on Moral Theology: Ethics and the Crisis in the Church. *Theological Studies* 66:117-136.

Keenan JF. 2010. *A History of Catholic Moral Theology in the Twentieth Century: From Confessing Sins to Liberating Consciences*. London: Continuum International Publishing Group.

Lakeland P. 2004. *The Liberation of the Laity: in Search of an Accountable Church*. New York, NY: The Continuum International Publishing Group.

Lawler P. 2010. *The Faithful Departed: the Collapse of Boston's Catholic Culture*. New York, NY: Encounter Books.

Lembo T. 2007. *The Hopeville Fire Department: a Boy's Tale of Betrayal by One of New England's Most Notorious Priests*. Doylestown, PA: Prose & Pictures, Inc.

Littleton J & Maher E. 2010. *The Dublin/Murphy Report: a Watershed for Irish Catholicism?* Dublin: Columba Press.

Lord Nolan, Swinton T, Abrahams C et al. 2001. A Programme for Action: Final Report of the Independent Review on Child Protection in the Catholic Church in England and Wales. Catholic Bishops' Conference of England and Wales. Available from: <http:\\www.bishop-accountability.org/resources/resource-files/reports/Nolan-Report.pdf > (accessed 25 January 2012).

Lothstein LM. 2004. Men of the Flesh: the Evaluation and Treatment of Sexually Abusing Priests. *Studies in Gender and Sexuality* 5(2):167–195.

Lytton TD. 2008. *Holding Bishops Accountable: How Lawsuits Helped the Catholic Church Confront Clergy Sexual Abuse*. Cambridge, MA: Harvard University Press.

McCormick R. 1999. Moral Theology 1940–1989: an Overview. In: Curran CE & McCormick RA, editors. *The Historical Development of Fundamental Moral Theology in the United States*. New York, NY: Paulist Press; pp.46-74.

McLaughlin BR. 1994. Devastated Spirituality: the Impact of Clergy Sexual Abuse on the Survivor's Relationship with God and the Church. *Sexual Addiction & Compulsivity* 1(2):145–158.

Murphy S. 2010. No Cheap Grace. *Studies: An Irish Quarterly Review* 99:303–316.

Myers JEB. 2006. *Child Protection in America: Past, Present, and Future*. Oxford & New York: Oxford University Press.

National Federation for Catholic Youth Ministry. 4 February 2012. NFCYM website. Available from: <http://www.nfcym.org/> (accessed 4 February 2012).

O'Gorman C. 2009. *Beyond Belief*. London: Hodder & Stoughton.

O'Hanlon G. 2010. The Murphy Report: a Response. *The Furrow* 61:82–91.

O'Malley JW. 2008. *What Happened at Vatican II*. Cambridge, MA: Belknap Press of Harvard University Press.

O'Meara NM. 2006. Rebuilding Community: Credibility, Sensitivity and Hope. In: Cahill LS, Garvey J & Kennedy TF, editors. *Sexuality and the U.S. Catholic Church: Crisis and Renewal*. New York: Herder & Herder Book/Crossroad Publishing Company; pp.7–17.

O'Meara TF. 1999. *Theology of Ministry*. Rev. ed. New York, NY: Paulist Press.

Papesh ML. 2004. *Clerical Culture: Contradiction and Transformation – the Culture of the Diocesan Priests of the United States Catholic Church*. Collegeville, MN: Liturgical Press.

Plante TG. 1999. *Bless Me Father for I Have Sinned: Perspectives on Sexual Abuse Committed by Roman Catholic Priests*. Westport, CT: Praeger.

Podles LJ. 2008. *Sacrilege: Sexual Abuse in the Catholic Church*. Baltimore, MD: Crossland Press.

Pope Benedict XVI. 16 June 2009. Letter of His Holiness Pope Benedict XVI Proclaiming a Year for Priests on the 150th Anniversary of the "*Dies Natalis*" of the Curé of Ars. The Vatican. Available from: <http://www.vatican.va/holy_father/benedict_xvi/letters/2009/documents/hf_ben-xvi_let_20090616_anno-sacerdotale_en.html> (accessed 25 January 2012).

Pope Benedict XVI. 20 December 2010. Address of His Holiness Benedict XVI on the Occasion of Christmas Greetings to the *Roman Curia*. The Vatican. Available from: <http://www.vatican.va/holy_father/benedict_xvi/speeches/2010/december/documents/hf_ben-xvi_spe_20101220_curia-auguri_en.html> (accessed 3 February 2012).

Pope Benedict XVI. 11 June 2010. Conclusion of the Year for Priests. Holy Mass. Homily of His Holiness Pope Benedict XVI. The Vatican. Available from: <http://www.vatican.va/holy_father/benedict_xvi/homilies/2010/documents/hf_ben-xvi_hom_20100611_concl-anno-sac_en.html> (accessed 25 January 2012).

Pope Benedict XVI. 19 March 2010. Pastoral Letter of the Holy Father Pope Benedict XVI to the Catholics of Ireland. The Vatican. Available from: <http://www.vatican.va/holy_father/benedict_xvi/letters/2010/documents/hf_ben-xvi_let_20100319_church-ireland_en.html> (accessed 24 January 2012).

Pope John Paul II. 30 December 1988. Post-Synodal Apostolic Exhortation: *Christifideles Laici*. The Vatican. Available from: <http://www.vatican.va/holy_father/john_paul_ii/apost_exhortations/documents/hf_jp-ii_exh_30121988_christifideles-laici_en.html> (accessed 3 March 2012).

Pope John Paul II. 12 March 1992. Post-Synodal Apostolic Exhortation: *Pastores Dabo Vobis*. The Vatican. Available from: <http://www.vatican.va/holy_father/john_paul_ii/apost_exhortations/documents/hf_jp-ii_exh_25031992_pastores-dabo-vobis_en.html> (accessed 4 February 2012).

Pope John Paul II. 11 June 1993. Letter of His Holiness John Paul II to the Bishops of the United States of America. The Vatican. Available from: <http://www.vatican.va/holy_father/john_paul_ii/letters/1993/documents/hf_jp-ii_let_19930611_vescovi-usa_en.html> (accessed 25 January 2012).

Pope John Paul II. 1997. *The Theology of the Body: Human Love in the Divine Plan*. Boston, MA: Pauline Books & Media.

Pope John Paul II. 22 November 2001. Post-Synodal Apostolic Exhortation: *Ecclesia in Oceania*. The Vatican. Available from: <http://www.vatican.va/holy_father/john_paul_ii/apost_exhortations/documents/hf_jp-ii_exh_20011122_ecclesia-in-oceania_en.html> (accessed 24 January 2012).

Pope John Paul II. 30 April 2001. *Sacramentorum Sanctitatis Tutela* (English Translation). Bishop Accountability org. Available from: <http://www.bishop-accountability.org/resources/resource-files/churchdocs/SacramentorumAndNormaeEnglish.htm> (accessed 3 March 2012).

Pope John Paul II. 16 October 2003. Post-Synodal Apostolic Exhortation: *Pastores Gregis*. The Vatican. Available from: <http://www.vatican.va/holy_father/john_paul_ii/apost_exhortations/documents/hf_jp-ii_exh_20031016_pastores-gregis_en.html> (accessed 3 March 2012).

Pope Paul VI. 21 November 1964. Dogmatic Constitutions on the Church: *Lumen Gentium*. The Vatican. Available from: <http://www.vatican.va/archive/hist_councils/ii_vatican_council/documents/vat-ii_const_19641121_lumen-gentium_en.html> (accessed 24 January 2012).

Pope Paul VI. 25 July 1968. Encyclical Letter *Humanae Vitae*. The Vatican. Available from: <http://www.vatican.va/holy_father/paul_vi/encyclicals/documents/hf_p-vi_enc_25071968_humanae-vitae_en.html> (accessed 12 February 2012).

Pope S. 2006. Descriptions and Prescriptions: Proposed Remedies for a Church in Crisis. In: Cahill LS, Garvey J & Kennedy TF, editors. *Sexuality and the U.S. Catholic Church: Crisis and Renewal*. New York, NY: Herder & Herder Book/Crossroad Publishing Company; pp.183–195.

Price D. 2008. *Altar Boy, Altered Life: a True Story of Sexual Abuse*. Indianapolis, IN: Dog Ear Publishing, LLC.

Radcliffe (O.P.) T. 2010. Come to Me All You Who Labour. In: Littleton J & Maher E, editors. *The Dublin/Murphy Report: a Watershed for Irish Catholicism?* Dublin: Columba Press; pp.17–28.

Richter (1808–1864) AL, Gratian (12th C), Church of Rome & Pope Boniface VIII (1295–1303) et al. 2012. *Corpus Juris Canonici* (1879). University of Toronto Internet Archive. Available from: <http://www.archive.org/details/corpusjuriscanon00richuoft> (accessed 25 January 2012).

Rigali N. 1998. On the *Humanae Vitae* Process: Ethics of Teaching Morality. *Louvain Studies* 2:3–21.

Rigali N. 2007. Moral Theology and Church Responses to Sexual Abuse. *Horizons* 34(2):183–204.

Rigert J. 2008. *An Irish Tragedy: How Sex Abuse by Irish Priests Helped Cripple the Catholic Church.* Baltimore, MD: Crossland Press.

Robinson G. 2008. *Confronting Power and Sex in the Catholic Church: Reclaiming the Spirit of Jesus.* Collegeville, MN: Liturgical Press (originally published October 15, 2007, by Columba Press).

Rolheiser R. 1999. *The Holy Longing: the Search for a Christian Spirituality.* 1st in the U.S.A. ed. New York, NY: Doubleday.

Rosetti SJ. 1990. *A Tragic Grace: the Catholic Church and Child Sexual Abuse.* Collegeville, MN: Liturgical Press.

Salzman TA. 2008. *The Sexual Person: Toward a Renewed Catholic Anthropology.* Washington, DC: Georgetown University Press.

Schuth K. 1999. *Seminaries, Theologates, and the Future of Church Ministry: an Analysis of Trends and Transitions.* Collegeville, MN: Liturgical Press.

Schuth K. 2011. Assessing the Education of Priests and Lay Ministries: Content and Consequences. In: Lacey MJ & Oakley F, editors. *The Crisis of Authority in Catholic Modernity.* New York, NY: Oxford University Press; pp.317–348.

Steinfels P. 2003. *A People Adrift: the Crisis of the Roman Catholic Church in America.* New York, NY: Simon & Schuster.

The Editors. 7 June 1985. Priest Child Abuse Cases Victimizing Families; Bishops Lack Policy Response. National Catholic Reporter. Available from: <http://www.natcath.org/crisis/070585b.htm> (accessed 3 March 2012).

The General Counsel of the United States Conference of Catholic Bishops. 1988. USCCB Pedophilia Statement. *Origins* 17:624.

The Holy Roman Catholic Church. 2012. *Catechism of the Catholic Church.* The Vatican. Available from: <http://www.vatican.va/archive/ccc_css/archive/catechism/ccc_toc.htm> (accessed 3 March 2012).

The Investigative Staff of the Boston Globe. 2002. *Betrayal: the Crisis in the Catholic Church.* Boston, MA: Little, Brown and Company.

Traina C. 2003. Sex in the *City of God. Currents in Theology and Mission* 30:5–19.

Treacy B. 2010. Learning with Pope Benedict. *Doctrine and Life* 60(5. May–June):2–3.

United States Conference of Catholic Bishops. 1992. The Five Principles to Follow in Dealing with Accusations of Sexual Abuse. USCCB Office of Media Relations. Available from: <http://old.usccb.org/comm/kit4.shtml> (accessed 25 January 2012).

United States Conference of Catholic Bishops. 2002. Charter for the Protection of Children and Young People. United States Conference of Catholic Bishops. Available from: <http://www.usccb.org/issues-and-action/child-and-youth-protection/charter.cfm> (accessed 25 January 2012).

United States Conference of Catholic Bishops. 2006. Program of Priestly Formation (5th Edition). USCCB website. Available from: <http://old.usccb.org/vocations/ProgramforPriestlyFormation.pdf> (accessed 2 April 2012).

Vella JK. 2002. *Learning to Listen, Learning to Teach: the Power of Dialogue in Educating Adults*. Rev. ed. San Francisco, CA: Jossey-Bass.

VIRTUS Online. 2012. A program and service of The National Catholic Risk Retention Group, Inc. Available from: <http://www.virtus.org/virtus/> (accessed 4 February 2012).

Weigel G. 2002. *The Courage to Be Catholic: Crisis, Reform and the Future of the Church*. New York, NY: Basic Books.

West C. 2003. *Theology of the Body Explained: a Commentary on John Paul II's "Gospel of the Body"*. Boston, MA: Pauline Books & Media.

Wilson GB. 2008. *Clericalism: the Death of the Priesthood*. Collegeville, MN: The Liturgical Press.

Winter GA, Commission of Enquiry into the Sexual Abuse of Children by Members of the Clergy & Archdiocese of St. John's. 1990. *The Report of the Archdiocesan Commission of Enquiry into the Sexual Abuse of Children by Members of the Clergy – Volume I*. St. John's, NL: Archdiocese of St. John's.

Winter GA, Commission of Enquiry into the Sexual Abuse of Children by Members of the Clergy & Archdiocese of St. John's. 1990. *The Report of the Archdiocesan Commission of Enquiry into the Sexual Abuse of Children by Members of the Clergy – Volume II: Conclusions and Recommendations*. Saint John's, NL: Archdiocese of St. John's.